ECONOMIC PERSPECTIVES

ECONOMIC PERSPECTIVES

Further Essays on Money and Growth

BY
JOHN HICKS

CLARENDON PRESS · OXFORD
1977

Oxford University Press, Walton Street, Oxford OX2 6DP

OXFORD LONDON GLASGOW NEW YORK
TORONTO MELBOURNE WELLINGTON CAPE TOWN
IBADAN NAIROBI DAR ES SALAAM LUSAKA ADDIS ABABA
KUALA LUMPUR SINGAPORE JAKARTA HONG KONG TOKYO
DELHI BOMBAY CALCUTTA MADRAS KARACHI

British Library Cataloguing in Publication Data

Hicks, *Sir* John Richard
    Economic perspectives.
    1. Economics – Adresses, essays, lectures
    I. Title
    330'.08   HB171

ISBN 0-19-828407-1

*Set by Hope Services, Wantage, and
Printed in Great Britain by
Fletcher & Son Ltd., Norwich*

PREFACE (AND SURVEY)

All of the essays that are collected in this volume have been written during the last twelve years. Most of them have been published previously, in different journals (no two in the same journal), so that few people, except the author, will ever have read them together. But there are two, the long Essay III, and also Essay VIII, which have not been published before. During those same twelve years I have published five other books: *Capital and Growth* (Oxford 1965), *Critical Essays on Monetary Theory* (Oxford 1967), *A Theory of Economic History* (Oxford 1969), *Capital and Time* (Oxford 1973), *The Crisis in Keynesian Economics* (Yrjo Jahnsson lectures, Blackwell 1974). Though the subjects of these books, and the methods of approach that are adopted in them, are superficially different, it is my belief that they belong together, and fortify one another. When the present essays are looked at with them, that may become clearer. But it will doubtless also help if in this preface I attempt a brief statement of the point of view which they, and these essays, have in common.

I must begin with negations. They gave me a Nobel prize (in 1972) for my work on 'general equilibrium and welfare economics', no doubt referring to *Value and Capital* (1939) and to the papers on Consumers' Surplus which I wrote soon after that date.[1] This is work which has become part of the standard literature of what is called in modern controversy 'neo-classical economics'. But it was done a long time ago, and it was with mixed feelings that I found myself honoured for that work, which I myself felt myself to have outgrown. How that has been I shall try to explain.

What I now think about *Value and Capital* is the following. The 'static' part, with which it begins, is an elaboration of Paretian demand theory, taking step after step along a road

[1] The most important of them being 'A Rehabilitation of Consumer's Surplus' (Review of Economic Studies 1941, reprinted in Arrow and Scitovsky, *Readings in Welfare Economics*).

which seemed pre-ordained as soon as one had taken the first step (that taken in the 1934 article which I wrote with Roy Allen[2]). The vistas that opened up were in their way exciting; so it was difficult when writing not to exaggerate their importance. Thus it was that I perpetrated the too well-known sentence in which I so preposterously exaggerated the importance of the perfect competition assumption, declaring that its abandonment would involve the 'wreckage . . . of the greater part of economic theory'.[3] I should have said 'the greater part of the particular piece of theory with which I was at the moment concerned'.

In spite of all that has since happened to that particular piece of theory—the further elaborations at the hands of Samuelson, of Debreu and of so many others, not to speak of the econometric applications that have been found for it—the time came when I felt that I had done with it. But what I really regretted was that it had played so large a part as it did in the other part, the so-called 'dynamic' part, of *Value and Capital*.

The way in which I began in setting up that 'dynamic' problem I still feel to be right. The concentration on what happens in a particular period (my 'week'), a period which is recognised as being embedded in a historical process, so that it has *past* and *future*; the effect of past decisions, now become immutable, upon the form of the capital stock that has been inherited from the past; the effect of expectations of the future in determining the present form of capital investment; all this is right, and all this I would still maintain. Where I now feel that I went wrong was in my attempt to represent the markets of that week as being in equilibrium, even in 'general equilibrium', in the sense of my static theory. So long as one's model is operating under *given* expectations of the future, to do this is logically defensible; but since (as I already perceived) the week should be no more than a step towards the analysis of a process, to work with given expectations is not enough.

[2] 'A Reconsideration of the Theory of Value' (Economica 1934).
[3] *Value and Capital*, p. 84.

So I tried to go further, to allow for the effects of current transactions on expectations; supposing that these effects could (somehow) be contemporaneous with the transactions themselves, so that an equilibrium which matched supplies to demands, at prices which allowed for the effect on expectations of those same prices, could be reached. That however was nonsense. In *Capital and Growth*, when I went over the same ground again[4], I could see that it was nonsense. 'It does deliberate violence to the *order* in which in the real world (in *any* real world) events occur.'[5]

It was this device, this indefensible trick, which ruined the 'dynamic' theory of *Value and Capital*.[6] It was this that led it back in a static, and so in a neo-classical, direction.

Since then, in the writings that are collected in this book, and in most of those which were listed at the beginning of this preface, I have endeavoured to avoid the relapse into statics. I have endeavoured to keep my thinking more securely in time, concerning myself with processes, but not just concerning myself with processes. It is not enough to think in terms of time-series. The time-units must be linked together and they must be linked in time, future becoming present, and present becoming past, as time goes on. One must assume that the people in one's models do not know what is going to happen, and know that they do not know just what is going to happen. As in history! It was helpful to go to history, even to diplomatic history and to military history, to remind one of what one had to mean.

What has just been described is the main thing which distinguishes my later work (or most of my later work) from

[4] The first nine chapters of *Capital and Growth* contain my principal methodological study of what is now called 'Microfoundations of macroeconomics'. I think I still stand by nearly everything in them. They are much more important than the exercises that are contained in the latter part of that book.

[5] *Capital and Growth* p. 73.

[6] It was a more serious source of damage than the assumption of single-valued expectations (certainty-equivalents) for which this same theory has often been criticised. See *Capital and Growth* pp. 70–71.

what I did at the *Value and Capital* stage. But I cannot tell the whole story in terms of my own work, in isolation. The issue was much bigger than that. For there was something curiously parallel to my own experience which had happened to Keynes.

What in Keynes corresponds to my *week* is his *short period*. Like my week, it has a past and a future. Its past is embodied in its given initial capital; its future is represented by given expectations, which are wrapped up in his Marginal Efficiency of Capital schedule. Subject to these data, the system is supposed to be in equilibrium, with desired demands and supplies being equal at the ruling prices in all markets (except the labour market). It is because the system is supposed to be in equilibrium during the short period (everything about the process by which that equilibrium is attained being neglected) that an analysis, which is formally quite similar to neo-classical static analysis, can be applied to it. It was this formal model of Keynes which I myself summarised in the ISLM diagram.[7] There is indeed much more in the *General Theory* of Kenyes than this formal model, and very much more in some of Keynes's other writings, which can quite properly be used to elucidate his work. I am nevertheless convinced that those later writers (so many later writers!) who have taken their Keynes from the ISLM diagram have indeed taken over what is one of the elements in what Keynes said.[8] But it is not enough; it is again a relapse into statics.

Once one recognises that it is not enough (neither ISLM nor the *Value and Capital* device is enough) one has to look more closely at what is supposed to happen within the period. Though so much more has to happen in Keynes's short period than in my week, it seems to have emerged that it is the week which throws up the issue more sharply. The week, in any case, has got to be straightened out first.

The main things which happen within the week are trans-

---

[7] 'Mr. Keynes and the Classics' (Econometrica 1937); reprinted in *Critical Essays.*

[8] See below, pp. 144–6.

actions.[9] So the working of the economy, within the week, should be a matter of the structure of markets. What kind of market should one be assuming?

There has fallen, on some of those who have got that far,[10] the shadow of Walras. General equilibrium goes back to Walras; how Walras think that his markets (his competitive markets) worked? Who fixes prices? Who, that is to say, decides that a price is to be changed? Walras did face that question; but the answer which he gave to it was quite peculiar. Actual transactors, he was saying, do not make prices; they accept them. So the prices must be made by someone else, by some independent functionary.[11] But how was such a functionary to be brought into existence? He did not explain.

My own approach to the issue has also been historical; but I began by thinking about Marshall[12] rather than Walras. How did Marshall suppose that a competitive market worked? His answer was less explicit, but (so far as I could reconstruct it) it seemed less peculiar. The key figure was the merchant, wholesaler or shopkeeper, who buys in order to sell again. He must therefore have a buying price as well as a selling price; but one could understand that in a competitive market, competition between merchants would 'normally' keep the margin between these two prices fairly small. (The narrowness of the margin would be the sign of a *highly* competitive market.) It

[9] In what follows I take these to be spot transactions, as seems to be the usual practice of economists – justified, I suppose, on the ground that forward transactions are no more than a form of risk-reduction, which (like insurance) may as a first approximation be left out. It may nevertheless be contended that when organised markets (see below) are brought in such a procedure is dangerous; and there are parts of the *General Theory* which can be read as an indication that this was Keynes's own view. Keynes's work in this field was carried further by Kaldor ('Speculation and Income Stability', originally 1939, reprinted in his *Essays* in a much revised form). Recent work by Paul Davidson follows in a similar track. I have not pursued it myself, since some tentative pages in *Value and Capital*.

[10] I think of Clower, and of Leijonhufvud, and perhaps of Patinkin.

[11] Clower calls him an 'auctioneer' but I don't think he is an auctioneer.

[12] *Capital and Growth* ch. 5, 'The method of Marshall'.

would then be the merchant who would play the part of Walras' functionary; it would be he who would make prices, raising them *or lowering them*, whenever he saw a change of making a profit on a particular transaction. All that the manufacturer (or ultimate seller) could do would be to accept or refuse the price that was offered to him; though he could refuse, on occasion, for fear of 'spoiling the market' (as Marshall says). Thus it would be the merchant who would keep the market 'atomistic'.

It seemed reasonable to suppose that in Marshall's day a market which was roughly of this type would have been the commonest type of market; though one could understand how it would be that within a system of markets of this character, another type of market could arise. This is that which has been called the *organised market*, a type which has in fact long existed. Organised markets are like Walrasian markets, in that they work under rules; but the rules are rules of a club. Access to such a market must be restricted, to those who promise to keep the rules, and who are willing to pay the costs of administering them (dealing for instance with disputes about them). The club, if it chooses, can employ a Walrasian functionary; or it can organise dealings in other ways. Organised markets commonly appear when a group of traders have become habituated to trading with one another. They are formed because it is discovered that to work under rules diminishes the costs of making transactions. Transaction costs, it will be noticed, have to brought in.

I tried the hypothesis that a system of this kind—unorganised markets, with prices made by merchant intermediaries, not excluding the appearance of organised markets in particular conditions where they were found to be suitable—had been the dominant market form throughout most of history; my *History* book is largely an endeavour to try that out. The matter needs much more investigation; but, so far as I could see, the hypothesis worked fairly well. There would however be no implication, on this historical approach, that such a market form is inevitable. If it seemed to fit the remoter history, it must surely, in the present century, have markedly declined. It has been largely replaced by what I have called *fixprice* markets, in which prices are set by the producers themselves (or by some authority); so they are *not* determined by supply and demand. It is of course granted that cost conditions, and sometimes also demand conditions, affect the prices that are fixed; but when these change, prices do not change automatically. Decisions, which are influenced by many other things that the simple demand-supply relationship, have to be made about them. Organised markets, which are more competitive markets, so that they do work, on the whole, in a recognisably supply-demand manner, remain in existence in some particular fields; but the unorganised flexprice market, the old type, is on the way out.

That modern markets are predominantly of the fixprice type hardly needs to be verified. It is verified by the most common observation. What may well be found more surprising is my contention that this is, on the long view, a new phenomenon. Yet it is easy to point to a number of developments which have favoured its growth in the twentieth century, but which cannot have been so important earlier. One of them (which is readily intelligible within the bounds of neo-classical economics) is the increasing scope of large-scale economies—the 'growth in the size of the firm'—which itself makes the atomistic type of market harder to operate.[13] Another, to which I myself would attach equal importance, is standardisation (branding and packaging), the ability of the producer, using modern technology, to give a quality imprint. Standardisation of quality, and standardisation of price, have a strong inclination to go together; for the cut-price article is brought under suspicion of inferior quality. It is a consequence of the standardisation that the role of the merchant is diminished; so that he becomes a mere outlet for the wares of the producer, without the power

[13] In Essay III (p. 101) I mainly rely upon this first cause; but that is a simplification. See however the note on p. 103.

of initiative that his predecessor possessed.[14] These things happen, it will be noticed, for technological, not for social or political reasons; thus they are likely to happen in any industrial, or industrialising, country, whether it is socialistic in its politics or not.

If one is right that there has been this change; it is a great change, even a revolutionary change. It may even be said that it carries the 'Keynesian revolution' along with it. One can certainly see its reflection in Keynes's own work. In the *Treatise* he is still Marshallian, thinking of prices as being determined in the old, universally flexprice, manner; this means that monetary influences act first on prices, and only as a consequence of price-changes do they affect output and employment. In the old type of market that is right; so we are not to criticise the older economists for having thought in that way; in their time, it is probable, they were quite right to do so. In the *General Theory* Keynes is moving towards a more modern world, though the transformation in his vision is not complete. He has not grasped that it is a change in market form that is at issue; though he does draw, from the change, many of the consequences which follow from it. He sees, in particular, that in a fixprice system the direct effects of monetary changes are on output and employment; and that the effects on prices (including wages) follow from them, in ways that are much less automatic.[15] And that, when one thinks it through, was perhaps the main thing that had to be said.

Yet if only it had been possible for Keynes to have set it in this context! We might then have been spared the excesses of those modern monetarists, who still live in their thinking in the old, universally flexprice, world; and who yet think that they can invoke Keynes's authority, or some part of his authority, for policies that still amount to 'leave it to the

[14] There is indeed the other alternative, that it is the distributor who gives the quality imprint, as does indeed happen with some large-scale chain stores. This is probably less 'fixprice' in its effects, but the tendency is there all the same.

[15] The working of fixprice markets is discussed in *Capital and Growth*, ch. 7. See also *Crisis*, p. 22 ff; and below, pp. 100 ff.

price-mechanism', policies which may well have been appropriate to that world but are not to its successor. And we might also have been spared the folly of some 'neo-Keynesians', who think only in terms of employment and output, and are prepared to let prices go hang! It is just because we do not live in a world of the old type that prices, money prices, do matter. Not just wages, but many other prices also, have social functions as well as economic functions. In a fixprice world, in which so many prices are administered, and have to be administered, the social functions have become more important, and more sensitive, than they were.[16]

If the *General Theory* had been set in this context, the model (or rather the principal model) that was used in it could have been represented as consisting of fixprice markets (for labour and for commodities) together with just one flexprice market, the market for bonds. On that arrangement, the single financial market must have a special relation with money. In reality, of course, there are many financial markets, and the relation between them and money is less simple than it appears to be in Keynes. Thus there was much in monetary theory (even in quite a narrow sense of monetary theory) which Keynes left to be done.

One of those problems—the relation between short and long rates of interest—I did try to deal with in *Value and Capital*;[17] but though the work that was done on it there had some pioneering quality, it is so incomplete as to be misleading. (This was the place where my inadequate treatment of uncertainty did most matter.[18]) There is a much better treatment in *Critical Essays*;[19] but it owes as much to Hawtrey as to Keynes. It is my view that the work of Hawtrey in this field has been much underrated. How much (still) can be learned from him is described in Essay V below.

My own later work on money has appeared in three main

---

[16] See below, Essay IV; also *Crisis*, pp. 77-9.
[17] *Value and Capital*, ch. 11.
[18] See *Capital and Growth*, p. 71.
[19] See especially Essay V of that book, 'The Yield on Consols', pp. 92-4.

parts; (1) *The Two Triads* (included in *Critical Essays*). (2) *The Crisis in Keynesian Economics.* (3) Essay III in this book. Though these were written quite separately, they are, I believe, broadly consistent with one another. There are three principal themes running through them, to which attention may usefully be drawn.

(i) The rejection of the portfolio approach to transaction balances. 'The important thing about M_1 (*in Keynes's sense of M_1*) is that it is not voluntary, save in a very indirect manner. It is the indirect consequence of decisions taken for quite other reasons, with no direct calculation of their monetary repercussions. . . . It is the money that is needed to *circulate* a certain quantity of goods, at a particular level of prices.'[20] Such money may be regarded as an input into the productive process. In the short run, with given institutions, its input coefficient may well be fairly constant; but in the longer run, with technical innovation, it may be changed.[21]

(ii) Liquidity and flexibility. Even with respect to his M_2, I now reject the simple portfolio approach, because it is not sufficiently *in time.*[22] 'Liquidity is not a matter of a single choice; it is a mtter of a sequence of choices, a related sequence. It is concerned with the passage from the unknown to the known—with the knowledge that if we wait we can have more knowledge.'[23] This notion is quite consistent with much of Keynes's work on liquidity; but in the *General Theory* (perhaps because of the relapse into statics) it seems to have dropped out.[24]

[20] *Critical Essays*, pp. 15–16.

[21] *Crisis*, pp. 48–9.

[22] I do not mean to reject it for other purposes. I do indeed have a contribution to it which will be made in this book. It is Essay VIII, which I once thought of entitling 'A Suggestion for simplifying portfolio theory'. But I rejected that title, since the range to which the argument applied turned out to be wider.

[23] *Crisis*, pp. 38–9. I have corrected, in making this quotation, an obvious slip.

[24] It cost me much trouble to recover it. I was not clear about it when I wrote the second of the *Two Triad* papers (and still less when I wrote

(iii) It is incumbent on one, as soon as one rejects the Money-Bonds simplification, to construct a model of financial markets, showing, as explicitly as one can, the relations between them. I have made several attempts at such a model; that which is set out on pp. 75–80 below is perhaps the most usable. It should be capable of further development.[25]

All this, in spite of the practical issues that have come into sight with it, is formally no more than theory of a single period (*week* or *short period*). It gives no help in relating successive periods, in stringing periods together. Yet that is what has to be done if we are to have a theory of Growth.

There are many theories of growth; but there are three, in particular, on which I have worked myself. First of all, there is the completely 'neo-classical' production function theory, the theory which in my *Theory of Wages* (1932) I took from Pigou. I explain in Essay I of this book why I now reject it.[26]

Secondly, there is the steady state theory, which has taken many forms in the work of others, and of which I gave my own version in some later chapters (12–15) of *Capital and Growth*. Periods, in such a model, are linked together; but the price of the linkage is that the periods are made similar; each of them, in essential respects, is just like the rest. Such a long-period equilibrium, or growth equilibrium, is indeed a relapse into statics—a much worse relapse, I have come to feel, than ISLM. For there are presented, in the ISLM analysis, some aspects of a real situation; though, as we have seen, not enough. But the real world is not in a steady state, never has been, and

---

the paper entitled 'Liquidity' that was published in the Economic Journal, 1962). The correct statement is in *Crisis*, pp. 37–42. In Essay III of this book I carry on from that.

[25] My first attempt was in Chapter XXIII of *Capital and Growth* (a chapter which is really an appendix). My second was in the third part of the *Two Triads*. There is much in that third part, especially the distinction between Funds and Financiers, which I would want to keep.

[26] See also *Capital and Growth*, ch. 24; *Capital and Time* ch. 15; and for the historical origins of Pigou's 'materialism', Essay VII below. It will be noticed that the assumption of a homogeneous material capital enables the problem of linking the periods to be assumed away.

(probably) never can be. So the most that can be hoped from steady state theory is that it may provide some concepts with the aid of which we could say something useful about a changing world.

But when I went on to that, using the steady state model of *Capital and Growth*,[27] I found that it did not in fact much help. I did not at first see why. Then I came to realise that in spite of the linkages that had been provided, my model was still too 'materialist'.[28] It was too dependent upon the technical specifications of capital goods—goods which are only produced as intermediate products in the production of something else, so that their technical specifications do not signify. A truly dynamic model is encumbered by such specifications. It is freer to attend to the important things if it rides across them.

That is what led me to go back to the Austrians; and to develop a 'neo-Austrian' model in *Capital and Time*. I had to begin with an 'Austrian' form of steady-state theory, but that was no more than preparation. The important part of *Capital and Time* is its new theory of 'Traverse';[29] but even that is given no more than a very formal statement.

Essays I and II of this book are applications of *Capital and Time*. They belong to that book, and could have been included in it; but perhaps it is better that they should be placed here, for they should be understandable by readers who do not wish to work through the formal theory. Yet *Capital and Time* is the ladder by which I myself climbed up to the point of view that is represented in these essays; though I had to diminish my dependence on the formal argument before the point of view could be stated clearly. It is stated, in Essay I, in what are still rather theoretical terms, the point of view being mainly defined in relation to other theories. In the essay on 'Industrialism' the ladder has finally been kicked down.

Though there is this connection between 'Industrialism' and *Capital and Time*, there is also a connection between it and my

[27] *Capital and Growth*, ch. 16, on 'Traverse'.
[28] See again Essay VII below.
[29] Chapters VII–XII, and for further comment, pp. 190–5 below.

History book. It was remarked, by some readers of that book, that its 'story' went as far as the Industrial Revolution (in the conventional sense) but was very sketchy on what has happened afterwards. There was a last chapter which seemed to be missing. In the book[30] I apologised for not writing it on the ground that it would be 'out of proportion'; but that was just an excuse. My true reason for not writing it, at that time, was that I did not then possess a theoretical structure, in which I believed, round which I could write it. Later on, after *Capital and Time*, I thought I possessed it. So when I got the invitation (from Andrew Shonfield) to deliver a lecture, which should in substance be the missing chapter, I thought I could do it. How it came out will be seen.[31]

I have one thing to add, of more conventional prefatory material, before concluding this preface. During all of the twelve years, during which these essays (and the other writings on which I have been commenting) have been written, I have been a Professor Emeritus; but I have been allowed to continue to work at All Souls. I am grateful to the College for the privilege that they have given me, and I am particularly grateful that it has enabled me to do a little teaching, and so to have students with whom to work. I have been particularly fortunate in the helpers who have come to me in this way, during these years. There are three in particular, whom I would like to mention: Stefano Zamagni, now Professor in Parma, Italy; Klaus Hennings, now Professor in Hanover, Germany; and A.M. Courakis, now Fellow of Brasenose College, Oxford. To these I would like to add the name of Rainer Masera, now of the Bank of Italy, though his time in Oxford preceded the

---

[30] *Theory of Economic History*, p. 160.

[31] Some of the points that have been made in this preface are made, in a somewhat different way, in a paper I wrote for a Festschrift for Nicholas Georgescu-Roegen ('Some questions of Time in Economics' in *Evolution, Welfare and Time in Economics*, Lexington Books, 1976). Since it did not appear in that place until the present volume was in the press, it could not be included here. This preface partially, but not wholly, replaces it.

twelve years; for he made me re-think the structure of interest rates, and so left his mark on *Capital and Growth*, and *Critical Essays*. To the stimulus which I have derived from this circle of young economists I owe a great debt.

February, 1977   J.R.H.

CONTENTS

I THE MAINSPRING OF ECONOMIC GROWTH*

In my *Theory of Wages*, first published in 1932, there is a chapter (VI) entitled 'Distribution and Economic Progress'. It was the first to be written of the theoretical chapters in that book; so it is in a sense the first of my contributions to economic theory. I do not think much of it now; I think that I have learnt a good deal since I wrote it. It has nevertheless had a considerable progeny. Work that is based upon it, or on other constructions of the same character, continues to appear; so it is far from being dead. Yet I myself have moved away. It may be useful to take this opportunity of explaining how this has happened. It is not inappropriate to do so, since in doing so I shall describe what seems to be to be an important part of the work I have done, in all the time from 1932 to the present.[1]

It was characteristic of that approach, from which I began, that it treated the Social Product as being made by two Factors of Production, Labour and Capital; the services of Labour and the services of Capital contributing to the Product in much the same way. An increase in the amount of either Factor that was applied would increase the Product, *other things being equal*. With given amounts of Factors applied, there would be just so much Product; so (again other things being equal) there would be a Production Function (as it

---

* Nobel lecture (reprinted from the *Swedish Journal of Economics*, 1973).

[1] It is the duty of a Nobel prize-winner to give a lecture in Stockholm in which he is supposed to summarize his own work. Though the prize was given to me for work on 'general equilibrium' I preferred to trace the evolution of my thinking on capital, wages, and invention. This is of course a field in which many others have been working beside myself. How much I have learnt from others, especially, perhaps, from Roy Harrod, from Joan Robinson, and from Nicholas Kaldor, will I hope be apparent.

later came to be called) representing Quantity of Product as a Function of Quantities of Factors applied. The return, per unit, to each Factor was equal to its Marginal Product, which diminished as the amount applied of that Factor increased, the amount of the other remaining constant. It followed at once that an increase in the quantity applied of one Factor (that of the other remaining unchanged) would increase the absolute share of the Product going to the other Factor; but since the absolute share of the increasing Factor might be either increased or diminished (according as its Marginal Productivity curve was elastic or inelastic) the distribution of the Product between the Factors (relative shares) might be shifted either way. Which way it went would depend upon the 'shape' of the Production Function, a 'shape' which could be represented, as I showed, by what I called the 'elasticity of substitution'.

It was not supposed that the Production Function would remain unchanged over time; it would be shifted by the discovery of new techniques of producing—that is to say, by *invention*. Inventions, so Wicksell appeared to have shown (and I followed him), would not be adopted unless they raised the Social Product; but the shifts in the Production Function, due to invention, might be 'neutral', as far as distribution between the Factors was concerned, or might be biased either way. It seemed to me that rises in wages (rises, that is, in the share of the Product going to Labour per unit of Labour) would encourage the adoption of inventions which economized in Labour and so were biased against Labour; but whether such 'induced inventions' were to be regarded as shifts in the Production Function, or as substitutions within an unchanged Production Function, was left rather obscure.

The theory, which I have been outlining, has been decidedly influential; but almost every element in it has been a target for criticism. Some of the criticisms (such as those directed against the Marginal Productivity theory as such) can, I still believe, be rebutted, or partially rebutted;[2] but there is one that remains which I now feel to be decisive.

In the Production Function, 'Product', 'Labour', and 'Capital' are quantities; but it is necessary, if they are to be quantified, that there should be some means of reducing their obvious heterogeneity to some kind of uniformity. For none of the three is the reduction a simple matter; it cannot be solved, even in the case of Labour, by counting heads or by counting man-hours. The crucial problem, however, is that of capital.[3] Capital, here, must mean physical capital goods; it is an aggregate of physical goods which we have to represent by a single quantity. As is now well known (but was not so well known in 1932) there are just two cases in which this can be done without error—without any error, that is, for it is not denied that if either case is approached, without being actually reached, the error may be tolerable. One is the obvious case in which all components change proportionately; the other— which I myself may claim to have clarified in 1939—is that in which the price-ratios between the goods, or their marginal rates of substitution, remain constant.[4] In the former case the complex is representable by a number of physical 'bundles'; in the latter there is aggregation in value terms.

It is clearly impossible, in the case of the capital stock, to claim that the first of these conditions, in practical application, can be even approximately satisfied. For it is normal experience, in a progressive economy, that its capital, at the end of a period, contains different kinds of goods from those contained at the beginning. New items are introduced, and old items discarded. Only in a theoretical construct—a steady state—can proportions remain unchanged over time; and we can hardly make much use of that property, even for the

[2] As I have explained in the *Commentary* attached to the second (1962) edition of *Theory of Wages*, especially pp. 333–41.

[3] Crucial in the sense that it has been the major theme of controversy among economists. I accept that the aggregation problems, on the side of Product, are hardly less pressing.

[4] *Value and Capital* (1939), p. 33 and *passim*.

comparison of steady states, since proportions in one steady state will usually be different from those in another. There is little hope for a way out in that direction.

The other, at first sight, looks more appealing. Here, however, there is a more subtle objection, associated in particular with the work of Joan Robinson.[5]

If capital increases relatively to labour, other things being equal (so the Production Function theory appears to tell us), the marginal product of capital must fall, so the rate of return on capital must fall. But a fall in the rate of return on capital carries with it a fall in the rate of (real) interest, as a result of which the capitalized values of different goods (goods of different durability, for instance) must change disproportionately. So the marginal rates of substitution between them cannot be kept constant. The constant-price condition cannot be maintained; it involves a contradiction.

This does not mean that it is wrong for statisticians to value capital goods at constant prices—their prices, or costs or production, at some base date. Any practical measure of National, or Social Capital must I think be of this character. But a technological relation between Capital and Product, with Capital thus arbitrarily valued, carries no conviction; there is no reason why it should exist.[6]

All I have said so far is by way of preface. I have, on the whole, left it to others (since my early days) to live in the world of production functions and elasticities of substitution, between Factors globally defined. What I mainly want to talk about is a side of my work which has gradually developed over the years, and which, I now feel, is more promising.

It also goes back to that same *Theory of Wages*. I have so far been discussing Chapter VI; but there are other chapters (IX-X) where will be found the beginnings of quite a different

---

[5] 'The Production Function and the Theory of Capital' (*Review of Economic Studies*, 1954); and later writings.

[6] I have stated my present views on the Production Function at greater length in *Capital and Growth* (1965), pp. 293-305; and in *Capital and Time* (1973), pp. 177-84.

theory. These are curious chapters; their reception, when the book appeared, was much less favourable than that then accorded to Chapter VI. This was partly because the tradition in which I was working in IX-X—the tradition of Böhm-Bawerk and Wicksell—was much less familiar to English readers than that of Pigou, on whom I was drawing in VI; but mostly because of a head-on collision between what I was saying and the 'New Economics' which even then, three years before the *General Theory*, was already beginning to be the Economics of Keynes.

When I wrote the *Theory of Wages*, I was completely innocent of these ideas; I had scarcely a notion of what was going on at Cambridge, or for that matter in Sweden. But hardly had my book left my hands when I began to move in that direction myself. I stumbled upon something which, if not quite the same as Keynes's Liquidity Preference, has a close relation to it. And even before the *General Theory* appeared in 1936, I had begun to draw some of the consequences.[7]

There is much of my work which follows from that; this is not the place to describe it. I must keep firmly to the story of those chapters in the *Wages* book, and what followed them. The first result of the new point of view, when I reached it in 1933-5, was to make me deeply ashamed of what I had written in those chapters. I realized (too late) how inappropriate it was. It had nothing to do with the state of the world at the time when I was writing. I had diagnosed a disease, but it was not the right disease. The unemployment of 1932 was of quite a different character from what I had supposed.

It is nevertheless not useless to analyse a disease, even if it is not the disease which at the moment is unimportant. The time may come when one's work is more to the point. In my case, I think, it has come.

---

[7] 'A Suggestion for Simplifying the Theory of Money'. (*Economica*, 1935, reprinted in my *Critical Essays in Monetary Theory*, 1967). I have told the story of my "conversion" in 'Recollections and Documents' (Essay VI below).

The principal ground on which my chapters were attacked, in the thirties, concerned my initial assumption—that Trade Unions, or Government wage-fixers, can raise *real* wages. This, by Keynes and his followers, was in those days most resolutely denied. Trade Unions, they said, are concerned with money wages, not real wages. It is true that a rise in the money wages of a particular group will raise their real wages relatively to those of others; but a general rise in money wages, in a closed system, will simply result in a rise in prices in the same proportion, thus leaving real wages where they were. This of course implies that there is an elastic money supply. If the money supply is not increased proportionately, the rate of interest will rise; as a result of the rise in interest there will be a fall in the demand for labour. The cause of the unemployment is then identified as the inelasticity of the money supply.

It is fairly obvious, in these days, that this Keynesian argument is not so strong as it at first appeared. Directed, as it was of course at first intended to be directed, against the use of wage-cuts as a means of stimulating employment in depression, it retains its force. But it is much less strong on the other tack.

Though Trade Unions operate on money wages, it is surely in real wages that they are really interested. If a rise in money wages just leads to a rise in prices, they feel themselves cheated; so they return to demand another round of rises in money wages. Thus we get the cost-inflation, with which (during the last twenty and especially ten years) we have become so familiar. It could not occur without an elastic money supply; so why not put constraints on the money supply, and so check, or at least impede, the inflation? There are bound to be monetarists who will argue that way, and governments, in desperation, are bound to give some attention to them. Is the resulting unemployment then due to the monetary constraint, or to the wage-push which led to the monetary constraint being imposed? One can look at the matter either way, but it can well be argued that the latter way is the more fundamental.

So my 1932 analysis has come, at last, to some sort of contemporary relevance; but there is another kind of relevance, of which I had no suspicion when I wrote, but which has been there all the time. This is not a matter of analysing a disease; it is concerned with the normal growth, the healthy growth, of an economy. In healthy growth real wages should be rising. What are the consequences of that rise in real wages? My 1932 analysis was concerned with rises in wages off the normal path; but the rises that are on the normal path should have similar effects, though they will not include the causation of unemployment. Rather similar methods should be usable for their analysis; it should deepen our understanding of the growth process in general. This is the aspect in which I have lately been mainly interested. I will try to sketch some of the results I seem to have been reaching. This will be the subject of the rest of this paper.

I have talked all this time about those chapters IX–X of the *Wages* book, without specifying what they contain. Much of what they contain is detail, now irrelevant. There is just one thing that matters.

A rise in *real* wages, however caused, tends in itself to diminish the *real* rate of profit. This has two effects which work, in a sense, in opposite directions. One is to encourage the substitution of what are usually more capital-intensive methods; the other, because of the transfer of income from profits to wages, is to diminish saving. Far more is now known about both of these effects than I knew in 1932; but the distinction still holds. I will try to re-state it in a more modern form.

The first thing on which to insist is that it is quite unnecessary, because we use terms like 'capital-intensive' and 'rate of profit', to trouble ourselves about the valuation of the capital stock as a whole (as we appeared to have to do on the *production function* method). What matters is not the average rate of profit on the whole capital stock (which cannot be determined without such valuation); what matters is the

rate of profit on *new investment*. When the new investment is
undertaken, that profit is no more than an expected profit,
and what is realized may not be the same as what is expected.
It seems reasonable, however, if we are concerned with healthy
growth, to suppose that there is some broad concordance between what is expected and what is realized. Most ventures
come out more or less right. No more than that is required.

It cannot be profitable (in this sense) to make machines
unless the use of the machines is also profitable; so, to assess
the profitability of investment, we should look right forward
to the production of final product. In any production plan,
so considered, labour is input and final product is output; so
a rise in wages, in terms of final product, must diminish the
rate of profit on the plan, in terms of final product. To this
rule there is I believe no exception. It holds for any plan that
could be viable at the rate of wages in question.[8] So for any
plan (with inputs and outputs expressed in quantity terms)
there is a particular relation between (real) wage-rate and
(real) profit-rate, which can be drawn out as a downward-
sloping curve—what I now like to call the 'efficiency curve'
of the plan.

Next (though only provisionally) let us make the conventional assumption that 'technology' is given: that there are just
so many production plans, in the above sense, from which
choice can be made. Each such plan will have an efficiency
curve. Make the 'capitalist' assumption (I am not here concerned with the question of its justification) that the plan
which is actually chosen for new investment is that which gives
the highest return at the current rate of wages. It could be that
the choice was unaffected by the level of wages; but it makes
more sense to suppose that as wages change, different plans
(or techniques) will come to be the most profitable. There
will then be substitution along a 'spectrum of techniques' as
wages rise.

It is not the case (as used to be supposed) that there is any

[8] *Capital and Time* (1973), ch. II.

single physical index by which we can distinguish those techniques which lie 'further down' the spectrum from those which lie 'higher up'. There is no such index which can be employed without exception. I could already show (in 1939) that the 'Period of Production' that was used for this purpose by Böhm-Bawerk and Hayek will not in general serve.[9] But what is in substance the same argument can be used against any physical index, such as capital–labour ratio (when capital, by some device, is physically defined).[10] Yet we should not allow these refinements to obscure the fact that techniques which lie further down the spectrum (so that they require for their profitable adoption a low rate of profit, or interest) will *usually* be such as to involve higher preparatory costs, such as construction costs, as a means of economizing in running costs of production. We do not *usually* go astray if we think of such techniques as being in that simple sense more capital-intensive.

I shall later return to this substitution effect; for the moment I turn to the other, which is more troublesome. In *Theory of Wages* (as was natural at the date when it was written) I took the traditional view that more saving meant more capital accumulation, and that capital accumulation was favourable to rising wages. But in Keynes's system of thought, which was so soon to be sprung upon me, the effect of saving seemed to go the other way round.

The trouble was not (as might easily be supposed) that Keynes's theory was monetary, while my 'classical' theory was non-monetary. One can construct a 'barter' system, in which money plays no essential part, but which can still behave in the manner that Keynes identified. (It is not, incidentally, such an unrealistic construction; the world, in 1970-1, produced quite a good imitation of a Keynesian slump *in real terms*.) It has taken some time for this to be

---

[9] *Value and Capital*, ch. XVII.
[10] This is the principal point which the "re-switching" controversy is about. For further detal, see *Capital and Time*, ch. IV.

clarified—since Keynes himself, by unfortunate definitions which made saving and investment always equal, obscured the significance of a part of what he was saying.

If we make the distinction (which already in 1936 was familiar in Sweden) between desired and realized saving and investment, the issue becomes much clearer. In the desired sense there can be an excess of saving over investment, even in a barter economy; it will take the form of an undesired accumulation, an accumulation of surplus stocks. If there is an excess of investment over saving, in the desired sense, stocks will fall below normal, below what is desired; or surplus orders will pile up, orders which cannot be satisfied without abnormal delay. Such an excess, either way, may be regarded as a sign of disequilibrium which is perfectly possible, even in a barter economy.[11]

Saving–investment equilibrium, so defined, does not imply the Full Employment of Labour; for that also to be attained, further conditions are necessary. One of the conditions is that relative prices should be right. It is unnecessary, here, to discuss the vexed question whether it will always be possible, in a barter system with sufficiently flexible prices, to maintain both full employment and saving–investment equilibrium automatically. (I am myself convinced that it is not necessarily possible, but that is by the way.) What is important, for my present purpose, is that saving–investment equilibrium and full employment are different. One can suppose that there is saving–investment equilibrium, maintained continuously; and yet there can be unemployment, if the ratio of prices to wages is inappropriate. That is what I ought to have said in *Theory of Wages*. So interpreted, the Keynesian view and the 'classical' view fit together.

It has taken a long time to clear this up. In the central part

---

[11] The disequilibrium which in a closed economy is revealed by physical stocks is in an open economy mainly revealed by foreign exchange—the balance of payments. For foreign exchange, in a modern national economy, is the easiest stock to run down, or pile up.

of my *Contribution to the Theory of the Trade Cycle* (1950) I used what I have later called a *fixprice* model.[12] I introduced an equilibrium path—a saving-investment equilibrium path—and a full employment path which lay above it. I was interested only in departures from equilibrium; so the only function attributed to the full employment path was to act as a Ceiling, which imposed a constraint upon the disequilibria which could occur. I did not ask why the equilibrium path should lie below the Ceiling. Indeed, I said much too little about each. I just drew them as straight lines—which is a simple way of saying nothing about them!

The natural way of finding out more about them is to consider the possibility of maintaining *both* saving-investment equilibrium *and* full employment. Suppose that both conditions have to be fulfilled; what will be the consequences? Real wages, it is clear by now, will have to be flexible; can they be kept flexing always upwards? If they can, it may be that the simultaneous satisfaction of both conditions can be maintained without friction (this does not mean that it must be attained); if they cannot, if there must be fluctuations in real wages when both conditions are satisfied, there will surely be greater difficulties. To learn more about the *double-equilibrium path* (as we may call it) seems thus to be the next thing required.

It has been widely appreciated that it is the next thing required. Many (though by no means all) of the 'growth models' that have been developed on all hands during the last twenty years can be considered as answers, or attempted answers, to the question just put. Some of them, especially those labelled 'neo-classical', use the production function scheme I began by describing. I am myself untempted by that procedure, essentially for the reason given. It may nevertheless be agreed that the problem is a 'classical' problem; since we are putting disequilibrium behind us, what we have learned from

---

[12] See especially Chapter VIII of that book. Also *Capital and Growth* (1965), ch. VII-XI.

Keynes is for the moment irrelevant. It is to the classics that we must go for help. We shall find it, in my view, not in the 'neo-classics' but in the British Classical Economists, especially in John Stuart Mill.

When Mill 'abandoned the Wage Fund' he must have forgotten what he had said about it. (It is not surprising, in view of all the other things he had been doing, if by 1868 his recollection of his earlier work had become a little rusty.) In terms of the double equilibrium path, what is said in his *Principles* is substantially right. The wage-bill (the *real* wage-bill) is just the difference between final product and what is *taken out* of that product for other purposes. What is taken out will include not only 'consumption out of profits' but also the consumption of public bodies (as Adam Smith, when he was on this track, had been well aware). So long as the increment in this Take-out is less than the increment in final product, the real wage-bill must increase when final production increases. It must do so, along the double equilibrium path.[13]

We can at last begin to see how the substitution effect and the saving effect fit together. It is essential to hold fast to the behaviour of *final output*. This is the chain of causation: from investment to final output, from final output to wages, from wages to the rate of profit on new investment, and thence back on investment itself. There is much to be said of these steps. I cannot go into detail, but must confine myself to giving a general impression.[14]

Let us start from the making of an invention, which we had better think of as a major invention, so that the technique of production which it makes possible is much more profitable than any used before.[15] It needs to be embodied in new

[13] On Mill, see *Capital and Time*, pp. 58–62.
[14] There is a much fuller discussion in *Capital and Time*, chs. IX–X.
[15] In the case of an open economy, the opening of a new market for an export, or potential export, will have a similar effect.

equipment in order that it should be used; so without new investment it cannot be applied. But even if the invention had not been made there would have been some new investment; so the immediate result of the invention is that the technique which is embodied in new investment is changed. The rest of the economy proceeds more or less as before, using old techniques; they are now obsolescent, but they cannot be changed overnight.

The *new* processes will not produce final product at once; there must be a delay before the new equipment comes into production. During that delay, all final product comes from old processes; so (in double equilibrium) the old processes must continue in full production if final product is not to fall. Except by a fall in final product, no additional resources can be transferred to new investment; so it is just the resources which would have been employed in new investment, if the invention had not occurred, which can be transferred to the making of the new 'machines'.

It is by no means certain that final product will be increased even when the new equipment comes into production. For it may well be that the increased profitability of the new machines is simply a matter of reduction in running cost. They have no larger capacity than the machines they replace; it simply costs less to run them. There is then no rise in final output when the new machines come into production. What does happen is that resources are released; but if double equilibrium is to be maintained, they must still be employed. They may be employed in squeezing additional output out of old processes; or they may be employed in making new machines. In the former case, there will at that stage be a rise in final output; and even in the latter case, though there is again no increase in output while the extra machines are being made, there will *in the end* be an increase in final output. So it *is* true (as Wicksell supposed) that a profitable invention will always lead to an increase in final output; but it is perfectly possible that the increase may be long deferred.

Unless the rise in final output is absorbed by an increase

in Take-out, or has to be spread over too large an increase in the supply of labour, rising final output (when it comes) will mean a rising rate of real wages. (This is where substitution will come in.) But suppose for the moment that there is no substitution and no further *invention*. Investment continues on the same pattern as was established after the first invention occurred. Gradually, as old machines are replaced, the part of the capital stock which has become obsolescent will diminish; more and more will be of a 'modern' type. During all that time final product will be expanding, and wages rising. As wages rise, the rate of profit will decline, from the exceptional level reached just after the original invention, towards something more 'normal'. It will decline, though not before the modernization has been completed, to the level which is appropriate to a steady state under the new technique; for the level of wages which is established in that steady state is the highest that can be achieved (except by diminishing Take-out) so long as there is no substitution and no new invention.

We need not rely, to establish this conclusion, on the 'classical' view that a declining rate of profit will diminish the *incentive* to save.[16] Whatever be the nature of saving propensities, an approximation to a steady state is likely to occur, *if there is no further technical change*. It will be a different steady state, with a different distribution of income, according as saving propensities take one form or another. But it will always be a steady state; and in that state wages will always be higher and profit lower than they were on the way to it.

Now we can bring in substitution. If there is substitution along a spectrum of techniques—new techniques which would previously not have been profitable becoming profitable because of the rise in wages—the fall in profits will be slowed up. The effect of the substitution (in most cases at least) will be in the direction of adopting more capital-intensive techniques. These will probably, at their adoption, slow up the rise

[16] Nor even upon the sophisticated re-statement of the "classical" view that is due to Cassel (*Nature and Necessity of Interest* 1903).

in final product; and that probably means that they will slow up the rise in the rate of real wages. (Since they are directed towards economizing in labour, it is not surprising that they should slow up the rise in wages.) But—and this is vital—the result of the substitution will be to set the economy 'aiming' at a steady state with a higher final product per unit of labour, and therefore (with any reasonable behaviour of take-out) a higher level of wages. There are several ways of establishing this essential proposition;[17] the simplest, perhaps, is just to observe that in the steady state, when the system is fully adjusted to the new technique, every worker will have more 'capital' to help him when the method of production is more capital-intensive.

What I have just been giving is no more than an exercise; it does no more than distinguish one causal sequence which in actual experience will be crossed and mixed up with many others. It does nevertheless appear that this sequence may be rather fundamental. The mainspring of economic progress, it suggests, is invention; invention that works through the rate of profit. Each invention gives an *Impulse*, as we may call it; but the Impulse of any single invention is not inexhaustible. The exhaustion is marked by falling profit; but the cause of the exhaustion (on the Full Employment, or double equilibrium path) is scarcity of labour.

In saying this we are keeping, in substance, quite close to Mill. In Mill the 'declining rate of profit' is due to scarcity of land; but there is no reason in principle why the operative scarcity should not be any natural scarcity. Mill's view that the operative scarcity was land scarcity can only be regarded as empirical; it looked like being right at the time when he was writing, but over the whole time since then it does not look like being right.[18] The ultimate scarcity must be that of labour

[17] My own preferred way is that which is set out in *Capital and Time*, ch. X.

[18] But perhaps in our day it again looks like being right. See below, Essay III, pp. 99 ff.

or of land (or both); formally, it must be scarcity of some non-augmentable factor of production. There are of course many other scarcities which will arise in the working-out of the Impulse; but scarcities that can be overcome by investment will not reduce the rate of profit on new investment in general. They will shift the point in the productive process where the investment is to be made, but that is all. It is only the irre-movable scarcities which will ultimately compress the rate of profit.

Once we recognize that substitution, on the spectrum of techniques, is just one way of overcoming the scarcities that arise out of the Impulse, many things fit into place. If there is no technical change, following on the original invention, other than that which is directly implied by the invention, the Impulse which it gives will soon be exhausted. Scarce factors will then get the full gain which accrues to them from the original invention, but no more. But if there is substitution, directed towards economizing in those same scarce factors, the ultimate gain to them will be greater, and may well be far greater. There may still be a question of how the gain is dis-tributed between them. Taken together, however, they must gain in the end from the deferment of exhaustion.

It is of little importance, from this point of view, whether the substitutions are supposed to take place along an un-changed 'technology frontier', or whether they themselves partake of the nature of invention. The 'technology frontier', useful as it has been in the formation of the theory, and still (perhaps) indispensable in the first stages of presentation, is in the end a piece of scaffolding, that we can take down. The puzzles about 'induced invention' then give no trouble. We have just to define them as technical changes, the possibility of which is newly discovered in the working-out of the Impulse, and which are such that it would not be profitable to make them until the scarcities by which they are 'induced' have developed. They thus appear as secondary inventions, 'children' of the original invention, its 'economic children'; for we may surely allow it to have other 'children'—technical children, 'learning by doing' in a most extended sense—as well. The economies of scale, on which one school of economists lays such great stress, may well be introduced in much the same place. The great inventions will give great and long-lasting Impulses, because they have many 'children', of all these kinds.

It will clearly be difficult, in relation to contemporary experience, to draw a firm line between the primary invention and its 'children', when the latter are so broadly defined. Where the distinction is drawn is bound to be a matter of judgement, or of taste. In relation to earlier ages, where claimants to primary status are less thick upon the ground, the distinction may be easier.[19] One can certainly detect, in the nineteenth century, one major invention that gives a recognizable, and separable, Impulse—the railway. The Railway Age was an Impulse, the working-out of which is clearly visible, since there seem to have been at least a couple of decades in which no Impulse of comparable magnitude followed. Many economists (including sometimes Keynes) thought the Depression of the 1930s to be a Pause of similar character. That could be, but it does not have to be, since the Disequilibrium of the thirties can well be explained in other ways. It is impossible to tell its story without laying great stress upon the monetary aspect, which I have been disregarding; it may well be that it is right to tell the *whole* of its story in those terms. Yet there may be something more. It would be a great help if we knew, better than we do, if there was something more; for it would help us to understand the innovative process, as it works in this century, and so to know, better than we do, how far we can count upon steadiness in the flow of innovation. The study of past Impulses, with the aid of a better classification, might well throw much light upon this vitally important matter.

I return, in conclusion, to the *Theory of Wages* problem—

[19] These ideas were not fully formed when I wrote *A Theory of Economic History* (1969), but I was working towards them.

the consequence of maintaining a level of real wages which is higher than that which is appropriate for double equilibrium. After what has been said, we need not conceive of this problem in a static manner. The equilibrium wage-level may be allowed to be rising, but the actual wage-level is kept, all the time, somewhat above it. That this is a realistic problem cannot nowadays be denied; for the means that are available for the enforcement of such a wage-level are far more extensive than they were in the past. Granted this kind of a wage policy, what happens?

There seem to be two main cases. It is possible, in the first place, that the higher wage might be matched by a lower take-out. A lower take-out would raise the (real) wage-level that was consistent with double equilibrium; so the lower take-out should permit of the higher wage being attained without unemployment. So far, so good; it should, however, be noticed that if the course of the wage-level is established arbitrarily, fluctuations in take-out will probably be necessary in order to keep that arbitrary wage-level consistent with double equilibrium. The matter cannot be settled in this way once and for all.

Secondly, suppose that the higher wage-level is not matched by the lower take-out. I do not think it can be doubted that this also is a practical problem. For when we remember how much of the consumable product of modern economies is 'taken out' for social purposes, the demand for which comes from much the same source as the demand for higher wages, we must surely recognize that the alleviation which can come from lower take-out is likely to be limited. Say then that all that can be done in this direction has been done. Say also that saving–investment equilibrium is to be preserved. (It will not be easy to preserve it, but most of what is to be said under that head is well known; I need not enlarge upon it here). What, under these conditions, will be the course of the economy?

The higher wage, as we have seen, will affect the techniques that are chosen for new investment; we may take it that they will, on the whole, be more capital-intensive than they would otherwise have been, at corresponding dates. Such techniques will in the end raise final output, *per unit of labour employed*, more than it would have been raised by less capital-intensive investment. But, all along, the volume of investment (in saving–investment equilibrium) will be lower than it would have been otherwise. Thus, although the economy is 'aiming' at a steady state in which final consumable output, per unit of labour employed, is higher, employment along the path to that state (and—in principle—even in that final state) will be lower than it would have been. This, I now believe, is what I was trying to say in *Theory of Wages*; as will be seen, it is subject to many qualifications of which, when I wrote, I had no idea. But in substance the main point stands.

That it is possible for a 'developing' country, by choice of techniques that are too capital-intensive, to expand employment in its 'modern' sector less rapidly than it might have done, is nowadays familiar. What I am saying is little more than an application of that same principle.

II INDUSTRIALISM*

What does one mean by 'industrialism'? One thinks of it, of course, as the state of society that was brought into being by the Industrial Revolution. As a historical description, that will do; but if we are to look forward as well as back, we need something more than the starting-point of a historical epoch. Will that epoch terminate, or is it already terminating? Before such questions can even be considered, we need a different kind of definition. We have to make up our minds what it was that started in the Industrial Revolution; or, more strictly, which of the things that then started we are to regard as the main thing.

A recent paper by Professor Kuznetz[1] is of considerable help for this purpose. He defines not industrialism but what he calls 'modern economic growth'; this, however, is near enough to our 'industrialism' to give us something from which to begin. He defines his 'modern growth' by six characteristics, which, in brief and inadequate summary, are the following: (1) rapid increase in production and in population; (2) rapid increase in productivity—output relatively to input; (3) structural change, as exemplified by movement of population away from agriculture; (4) social change—urbanization and secularization; (5) revolution in transport and communication, making the world 'one world' as it was not before; (6) unequal growth between countries, so that some are 'advanced' while others are left behind.

* This was given as a Stevenson Memorial Lecture under the title 'The Future of Industrialism' at the Royal Institute of International Affairs, London, in November 1973 and was subsequently (April 1974) printed in *International Affairs*, the journal of that Institute. Reprinted by permission of The Royal Institute of International Affairs.
[1] S. Kuznetz, 'Modern Economic Growth: Findings and Reflections' (Nobel lecture 1971), reprinted in *American Economic Review*, June 1973.

There is nothing in Kuznetz's list, it will be noticed, about 'capitalism'. That I am sure, is right; it is right for his purpose, and will be for ours. Socialist countries industrialize, like 'capitalist' and 'semi-capitalist' countries; it is a world-wide phenomenon, not just one of the 'first', 'second', or 'third' world. So I have deliberately put industrialism into my title, not capitalism. Although there are many things which work differently in the two types of organization, the things which will most concern us are much the same.

These six characteristics of Kuznetz will have to be borne in mind; but they still leave us short of a unifying principle. What is the driving force behind these vast changes? Kuznetz's answer is, in his own words, 'the emergence of modern science as the basis of an advancing technology'. This looks like being the principle for which we are seeking; and in these days explanation in terms of science-based technical progress makes obvious sense.

Can we apply it, however, to the whole history of industrialism since, say, 1800? The science available in 1800 was of course quite rudimentary. Although one can trace a scientific element in most of the major nineteenth-century inventions, it is not suprprising that that element should be less conspicuous than it is today. There were indeed long periods in the general history of industrialism when technical progress did not seem to be very striking; so economists, looking for the causes of economic growth, felt that they had to explain it in other ways. One has only to go back to the 1930s to find a time when the importance of technical progress did not seem at all obvious. Few economists would then have given it the priority which now seems so natural. Neither to the traditionalists (now called neo-classics) nor to the Keynesians, in the beginnings of Keynesianism, did technical progress, in which they had little confidence, seem at all a sufficient explanation. It was mentioned, but it took a fairly subordinate place.

To the traditionalists, I think one may say, the driving force was accumulation of capital. By capital they meant physical goods, factories, and machines. Since they took it for granted that what was saved would be invested, the way to get more machines was by saving; so they attributed the rise of industrialism to the rise of a saving class. 'Every frugal man a public benefactor' had said Adam Smith. The explanation of historians, in terms of a 'Protestant Ethic', clearly fits in.

The Keynesians, of course, held that that was all wrong. It is not true, they said, that saving leads to investment: investment leads to saving. They had therefore to find their driving force in things which keep up the inducement to invest. These, in capitalist conditions, would be things which keep up the expected profitability of investment—the marginal efficiency of capital, as Keynes called it. His own list of the things which, he held, kept up the marginal efficiency of capital during the nineteenth century was: 'the growth of population and invention, the opening-up of new lands, the state of confidence and the frequency of war over the average of (say) each decade.'[2] Invention does appear, but it is secondary; the growth of population actually comes first.

Why was it thought, at this stage, that the growth of population is favourable to economic growth, in a broader sense? In a review which I wrote of the *General Theory*, on its first appearance, I tried to rationalize Keynes's contention. 'It does become very evident', I said, 'when one thinks of it, that the expectation of a continually expanding market, made possible by increasing population, is a fine thing for keeping up the spirits of entrepreneurs. With increasing population, investment can go roaring ahead, even if invention is rather stupid; increasing population is therefore actually favourable to employment. It is actually easier to employ an expanding population than a contracting one, whatever arithmetic might suggest—at least that is so when the expansion or contraction is expected, as we may suppose to be the case.'[3] So, with

[2] *General Theory* (London: Macmillan, 1936), p. 307.
[3] *Economic Journal* (June 1936), p. 252.

increasing population, expansion can proceed fairly easily.[4]

But today the population-induced expansion, envisaged at that time by Keynesians, looks much less appealing. For we look at it through the spectacles of the steady-state model, which in the economics of the 1950s and 1960s has become so familiar—a model in which there is just enough saving (and investment) to keep the expansion of equipment in line with the expansion of population, so that an increasing labour force works with a constant amount of equipment per head. One can see that in a steady state of that sort, the planning of production would be rather easy; so there would be no danger of a Keynesian loss of confidence, for everyone would know what had to be done in order that business ventures should come out right. That may be granted. But more than that is needed to explain what has happened; for a steady-state expansion, in which capital per head was constant and there was no technical progress, would show no gain in productivity. The expanded population would be absorbed, but that would be all. In such a steady state there would be no rise in real incomes and no rise in real wages.

But in this steady-state theory is there not an important element which is being neglected? Is it not the case that expansion as such, even population-based expansion, is favourable to productivity? 'The division of labour', we should have learnt from Adam Smith, 'is limited by the extent of the market.' By no subsequent economist has this been denied. In every work on economic principles there has been a section on increasing returns, or economies of scale, although in so much of our work it seems to take a back seat. For the moment there are just two things to be said about it.

First, what matters is the extent of the *market*. This is not

[4] I was less cautious on another occasion, when I suggested that 'the whole Industrial Revolution of the last two hundred years has perhaps been nothing else but a vast secular boom, largely induced by the unparalleled rise in population' (*Value and Capital*, p. 302). I quote from my own writings, as being nearest to hand; but it would not be hard to make similar quotations from what was written, at the time, by many authors.

a matter of the number of buyers; it is a matter of their purchasing power, their *real* purchasing power. An increase in population does not necessarily expand the demand for the sorts of goods in the production of which there are significant scale economies. An increase in the Indian population from 500 million to 800 million—which is what we are told may actually happen by the year 2000—would not necessarily, or even probably, make possible, in itself, significant scale economies in Indian industry. Nor does it seem likely that the increase in the British population, in the first half, say, of the nineteenth century, can have had an appreciable effect in engendering scale economies. It does not of course follow that scale economies are unimportant; but we must beware of driving them too hard.

Secondly, we must not be misled by Adam Smith's (essentially pre-industrial) pin-making example—his association of scale economies with specialization of labour. That is always one element; but is it not a characteristic of industrialism that it ceases to be the most important element? Labour, indeed, is potentially rather unspecialized; man, as a producer, has this enduring advantage over the machine, that he can do, or can learn to do, many different things. It is equipment—not all equipment, but most equipment—which is firmly specialized, being made to perform a particular job. So it is that there are short-run economies of scale in operating plant nearer to capacity; while long-run economies of scale usually imply new plant, adapted to the larger output. There is better adaptation of plant, which improves productivity.

These scale economies are embodied in plant; but are not the other improvements—those more directly due to 'advancing technology'—similarly embodied? It may be possible to find examples of science-based improvements which do not have to be embodied in physical equipment; but nowadays they are not at all easy to find, if the consequences of the improvement are looked at inclusively. The embodiment may be quite indirect. Not much in the way of industrial equipment is needed to produce the improved seed, which appears to be the operative agent in the 'Green Revolution'; but then we are told that its successful application needs concomitant use of extra fertilizer. So the improvement, as a whole, does require fixed equipment. The fertilizer factory is a part of the technical change.

Thus there is a rather central element in industrialism—or in 'modern economic growth'—of which we have not so far taken account. 'Science-based technology' certainly, but not just that; technology which needs for its application embodiment in physical equipment, or (in a very broad sense) in 'machines'. It has been obvious from the beginning that the machine is characteristic of industrialism; but it may not be so obvious that it is necessary for a definition.

There is, however, a further point. What drives the machines? For the first century of industrialism, the answer was coal; for the second century coal and oil, with a few other relatively minor fuels. This strict dependence upon a small number of particular natural resources, available at some points of the earth's surface but hardly at all at others, must surely be added as a key characteristic. One may dream of an industrialism which has cut itself free from this limitation; but it is hardly, as yet, even in sight. Economists, in their growth models, have tended to ignore this aspect; but their example can hardly be followed nowadays. Nevertheless, we will begin by considering the consequences of the embodiment in machines, a matter that is conveniently dealt with by simple economic analysis, and leave the question of power supplies to be dealt with later.

I shall now attempt to show some of the consequences which follow when industrialism is defined as 'science-based technical progress embodied in physical equipment'. Consider the story of some particular improvement, some particular technological 'advance'. There must clearly be three stages. First, a stage of research, the working-out of the idea. Secondly, a stage of construction, the construction of the equipment, the building of the 'machine'. Thirdly, a stage of utilization, in which the new productive power comes into operation.

In our day, during the last thirty years, the first stage, research and development, has become a major activity. But for most of the history of industrialism, this can hardly be said to have been so. Ideas dropped from Heaven; or, in less figurative language, they appeared as by-products of other activities undertaken for other reasons. They had little identifiable social cost; their economic effects could therefore be studied as if they came in from outside.

I shall begin by supposing that the idea does come in from outside, and that it is not too quickly followed by other comparable ideas, so that the effects of the single idea can be studied separately. There is indeed one example in history which more or less meets this requirement—the railway, that major nineteenth-century invention, so much more important, in its great days, than any other that was independent of it. The constructional stage and the utilizational stage, in the case of the individual railway, can be clearly distinguished; but for the railways as a whole the two of course overlapped. It took quite a long time to build a railway, but it took much longer to build all the railways. Why?

The most obvious explanation is that the resources available for railway building were limited. Any big constructional programme runs into bottlenecks—shortages of skilled labour and of materials, of which we may take as an example steel. These will slow up the programme at the outset; but as time goes on, they can be relieved. Labour can be trained and new steel mills can be set up, so that more steel can be produced. Thus while such constraints must be important at the outset, the time will come (and should come fairly soon) when they cease to be so important. They cannot sufficiently explain why the time to make *all* the new equipment should be so spread out. There must be other obstacles.

A possible obstacle is shortage of labour—labour in general, not specifically trained. In a particular country that may well be important; but for the world as a whole (and railway-building went on over the whole world) it does not look like being so important. Another is a monetary constraint; but that is a matter of particular institutions, and Keynes has taught us that it can be wished away. There still remains a further constraint, of which older economists were well aware; it is one which we have learnt from our own experience cannot be overlooked. It is the main reason why the application of a major improvement, such as the railway, is so long drawn out.

Let us suppose that the constraint of full employment is not operative; there are still some unemployed who could be set to work if opportunity offered. It is a pretty firm rule that if these unemployed are to be drawn into the productive process, they will have to be given wages which are greater than whatever it was they had been getting when they were unemployed. That must be so under any economic system, except in the case of slave labour; and it may be that even slave labour is no more than an apparent exception. Additional goods, on which these wages can be spent, will have to be provided; and who is to provide them? The goods that are currently available are the result of past production. (This is particularly obvious in the case of food.) Though more labour could be applied to producing more of these goods (since we are taking it that there is unemployed labour), it would take time before the goods were ready. So *at any particular time* the goods that are available for current consumption are fairly fixed in amount and are not very quickly extensible. The goods that are needed for consumption, out of the additional wages, must therefore in the short run be provided by someone else.

They might be provided by those who were previously saving doing more saving; but though this is a possible source, it cannot in general be counted on as a sufficient one. If it does not suffice, while employment is still pressed ahead, the goods will have to come from the real wages of other people. The ways in which that happens, if it has to happen, are well known. Under capitalism, there is a rise in prices relatively to wages. Both may rise in money terms, but wages lag behind prices. Under socialism, there is rationing, or there are queues or there is 'procurement'. Thus if voluntary saving does not suffice, there is involuntary saving. But the extent to which this is tolerable may be limited. It is likely to encounter resistance—in a poor country from farmers, who cannot easily be made to make involuntary savings; in a rich country from trade unions. In this sense there is a savings obstacle, which limits the possible rate of investment at any particular time.

It has been necessary to enlarge upon this obstacle partly because in the Keynesian teaching, on which the present generation has so largely been brought up, it is almost entirely missing. Keynes himself, writing at the time when he did, was probably justified in playing it down. For when one is dealing with recovery from a depression—the particular problem of the 1930s—it is not an important matter; for production during a depression is much below capacity and there are ample stocks of materials which can be quickly worked up into many sorts of consumption goods. Recovery therefore requires no more than a little involuntary saving. It is fairly safe, in that application, to leave it out of account. But this is just one of the ways in which Keynes's was *not* a *General Theory*.

The other is that I need it, very badly need it, for the elucidation of the more long-run changes with which we are here concerned. Let us return, for instance, to the question of population. It is in some of the poorest countries of the world that population is now increasing most rapidly. We are perhaps a little less worried than we were about the Malthusian peril—the problem of feeding the hundreds of millions of new mouths which demographers tell us will so soon be upon us. It is far from certain that we are right to be so complacent; but suppose we are right. We are still left with the problem of finding the savings in order to employ, in a 'modern' manner, even that fraction of the population of, say, India which is now employed in a 'modern' manner—a fraction which, with a larger population, will comprise many more people.

England, at the beginning of the Industrial Revolution, was

not, by the standards of that time, a poor country; and the same is true, as Kuznetz reminds us, of each of the other countries that have successfully industrialized. (He is inclined to regard Japan as an exception; I much doubt if, in the required sense, it is.) The necessary savings could therefore be secured fairly easily; and a rapid increase in population could after a fashion be accommodated. But it cannot be doubted that, in the English case at least, it was a strain. Do we not see a monument to that strain in the houses then put up in our industrial cities? If the expanding population kept up the spirits of businessmen, there were horrid things to be set on the other side.

I have been talking about the black side of the savings constraint; but there is a brighter side too. Although it sets a limit on the rate of expansion of investment that is possible *at the moment*, this is a limit which as time goes on should be progressively relaxed. For more and more of the new 'machines' will reach their utilizational stage. If, as we are supposing, the new technique is genuinely superior, genuinely more productive than what it replaces, the availability of the new equipment will enable production to be increased. Out of the larger production it will be easier to make savings. Thus at some time after first introduction, the ceiling which had been hitherto imposed will gradually lift. Even a single major invention, as it is carried through, will (so it appears) lift a hitherto stagnant economy into 'self-sustained growth'.

This is so (subject to the qualifications—the same qualifications—to which we shall be coming) whatever the organization of the economy. In the 'capitalist' model, familiar in economic textbooks, the improvement in productivity raises profits, and from the larger profits it is easy to make larger savings. Under socialism, the profits accrue to public bodies; but here again, if the new technique has proved productive, public profits will be increased, and from their larger profits the public bodies will find it easier to finance new investment. They may not do so, and the capitalists may not do so; but in either case there is some presumption that they will.

Obviously, in a limited world, the expansion that is due to a single improvement cannot go on for ever. If railway-building for example, went on for ever, the world would in the end become cluttered up with railways. The profitability, or productivity, of a railway depends on its location; the time must come when a new railway project which will yield any surplus over cost, must be hard to find. For unlimited expansion, of a particular kind, such as that induced by a particular invention, there is not enough space.

Space, however, is not the only issue. Any indefinite expansion must encounter scarcities. Some, such as the bottlenecks previously discussed, are removable; in time they can be overcome. Others—either by necessity, or in the world as it is and has been—are irremovable. It is by irremovable scarcities that expansions, such as we have been discussing, are brought to a stop.[5]

The first economist to see this at all clearly was Ricardo. Since, however, he worked it out only for a particular case (and not, as it proved, a very realistic one) it was many years before the significance of what he had shown was fully understood. He supposed that the supply of labour was indefinitely extensible; it would increase without limit, so long as subsistence for the increasing labour force could be provided; so his operative scarcity was scarcity of agricultural land. This was responsible for his 'declining rate of profit'. Because of the scarcity of land, provision of an unchanged subsistence for an increasing labour force would become more expensive from the point of view of the employer, even though there was no rise in the real consumption of the labourer himself. With labour costs rising, the rate of profit would fall.

In Ricardo's pure model, technology is unchanging; and this has caused much confusion. For he had not shown how it

---

[5] There is also the important class of scarcities which *in the end* are removable, but which take so long to remove that they impose a temporary check. These may well be an important reason for the fluctuations which in historical experience have accompanied industrial growth.

could be that the rate of profit initially would be so high that it was able to fall. If we start the story a little further back, with some major improvement that has lifted the rate of profit, what he said becomes much more intelligible. What he was showing was that if there is no further improvement in technology, the rate of return on the spreading of the original improvement must decline over time.

Scarcity of land for food production may have this effect; so may scarcity of land as a source of minerals, or of power, or for many other purposes. And so, it is of the greatest importance to notice, may scarcity of labour. It would make a great deal of difference—in the rather old-fashioned capitalist economy which Ricardo was of course assuming—whether the operative scarcity (or the main operative scarcity) was shortage of land or shortage of labour. In the former case (Ricardo's) scarcity of land would raise rents; but in the latter, the shortage of labour would raise wages. It is possible that in a socialist economy there would be less difference. If the rents accrued to the state, they could be channelled to labour in some form of social benefit. But it would still be true, even in the socialist economy, that irremovable scarcity (of land or of labour) would cause the rate of return on the spreading of the original improvement to diminish. In either case the *Impulse* of the original improvement would in time peter out.[6]

When it is so interpreted (or generalized), the Ricardian theory still holds; and I maintain that it is rather fundamental. It is perfectly true that in our day the flow of fresh improvements ('advances in technology') is incessant; but that does not mean that the Ricardian theory has lost its importance. Current improvements (the 'latest improvements') make for the moment little contribution to growth in current production;

---

[6] There is a theoretical examination of the Impulse concept in my *Capital and Time: a neo-Austrian theory* (Oxford: Clarendon Press, 1973), ch. X; and one (which is nearer to the use made of it in the present paper) in my Nobel lecture 'The Mainspring of Economic Growth' (Essay I above).

that mainly comes from the unexhausted Impulses of past improvements. Thus if technical progress were to come to a standstill and the flow of new improvements were to dry up, the growth in productivity would ultimately come to a stop, but not immediately; for the impulses which were unexhausted at the time the technical progress stopped would remain to be worked out. In the growing phase of the economy, such exhaustion (though a continual threat to expansion) is continually warded off by new discovery, generating new Impulses.

The individual Impulse has two dimensions, since it is spread out over time. Its size and its time-shape depend partly upon the nature of the improvement which has initiated it, partly on the characteristics of the economy in which it is carried through. Consider the case of an Impulse which is ultimately to be finished off by labour shortage. It is perfectly possible for such an Impulse to have a first part in which it is labour-saving; expansion can then proceed for some considerable time before any shortage of labour (due to this Impulse) makes itself felt. At that stage, before the labour shortage sets in, the rate of expansion will depend upon the characteristics of those who get the profits; the readier they are to save and invest the profits which are made, the faster the expansion will be. Later on, when the shortage begins to take effect, this unfettered expansion is cramped and held back; its pace will still be affected, as before, by entrepreneurial push, but the effectiveness of the push will depend upon the extent to which it proves possible to find ways of overcoming the shortage. These themselves are technical changes, but they follow from the original change; they are 'induced inventions'.

It may well be useful to think of the original advance as having a progeny of technical changes following from it. We can distinguish at least three kinds. First, there are those of a purely technical, non-economic character; as the original improvement is carried through and embodied in the equipment that belongs to it, opportunities for further improvements present themselves—'learning by doing'. Secondly, there are those which come in as economies of scale; the expansion of production, in itself, offers opportunities for technical changes. Our 'induced inventions' come in as a third kind.

In relation to my theme these induced inventions are of particular importance. For consider again the case of an Impulse where the operative scarcity is shortage of labour. In the course of the Impulse, wages rise; real wages rise; whether the rise takes the form of a rise in money wages, or of a fall in prices with little change in money wages, is a monetary matter with which I am not here concerned. At the conclusion of the Impulse, when its expansionary power has been in the end exhausted by the rise in wages, the rise in wages remains. If there was no further Impulse, and no induced inventions, the economy would settle down to a steady state, with production ceasing to rise, or rising no more than proportionately to such increase in labour supply as was occurring. The economy would have attained what Adam Smith called its 'full complement of riches'; but the higher real wages, which had followed from the now exhausted Impulse, would remain.

Suppose, however, that there were induced inventions, induced (as in this case they would be) by the rise in real wages, by the rise in wages relatively to product prices (as a whole). Such technical changes would be directed towards economizing in labour costs, and thus to reducing the scarcity of labour. They would therefore tend to slow up the rise in wages. But their other effect would be to prolong the life of the Impulse, postponing its exhaustion. The rise in wages, which would otherwise have ended earlier, could continue longer; and the wage that would be attained in the end would be higher than that which would have been attained at the earlier demise. This can be shown in several ways; the easiest is simply to observe that the individual worker would in the end have more capital equipment to work with when the process of accumulation continued longer.

We have here, I do not need to emphasize, a basic opposition. It appears as an opposition between capital and labour; but more deeply considered it is an opposition between the short-run and longer-run interests of labour itself. It is another way in which industrialization is liable to inflict involuntary saving upon labour; less damaging than the other kind, since its cause is rising real wages—it cannot occur except as a consequence of rising real wages—but serious enough, and damaging enough.

There is one more general point that needs to be made. Suppose that, for whatever reason, there is a slowing-up of the rate of growth, what will happen? Those who have been brought up on Keynesian economics will take a very pessimistic view. Investment will decline, relatively to saving (voluntary investment relatively to voluntary saving); and such a fall must lead to unemployment. That is how it appeared in the Keynesian 1930s; but with longer experience we must take a different view. Admittedly, there are countries where it would not be surprising to find a Keynes-type reaction. Japan, for example, has got organized on the basis of a very high rate of saving; so a decline in the rate of voluntary investment there might well have the the regular Keynes effect. In most Western countries, however, it is saving that is deficient; a decline in investment might require some readjustments, but on the whole it would make things in that direction easier. What would not become easier is the behaviour of wages. There is a good deal of evidence that a slowing of growth, leading to a slower rise in real wages than had become customary, has a powerful effect in causing wage-inflation. A rise in money wages does not give what was expected from it, since prices rise too; so the pressure is repeated. The case of Italy, after 1962, is perhaps the most striking; but analysis of the British case appears to give the same answer.[7] It is, on the long view, a transitional phenomenon; but it is a formidable corner to be got round.

I am now at last in a position to look forward. I cannot go

[7] See, for instance, Johnston and Timbrell, 'Empirical Tests of a Bargaining Theory of Wage Determination' (*Manchester School of Economic and Social Studies,* June 1973). The matter is further discussed in Essay III below, see particularly pp. 102-4.

far in penetrating the 'mists of futurity'; but I can at least break the subject up. I shall discuss it under four heads: (1) technology; (2) economies of scale; (3) land; and (4) labour.

(1) Technology—science-based technology

You will not expect me to have anything useful to say about the prospects for the advancement of science. I know very little about science; indeed, when one thinks of the myriad departments into which science is now divided, it is doubtful whether anyone exists who is competent to judge of the opportunities which may present themselves all along the line. But our question is not just one of the advancement of science; it is a question of the transmutation of science into technology—economically productive technology. On that there may perhaps be a little more to be said.

At the stage when ideas 'dropped from Heaven', the appearance of economically productive ideas must have been almost random. Yet one can understand why it was that there seems to have been a rising trend. Science, at that stage, was a luxury; it was pursued as an amusement, or as a cultural activity in which some gifted people were privileged to pass their time. Like other luxuries, it was income-elastic; with increasing wealth, the proportion of income that was spent upon it increased. Thus it was an expanding activity, and the stream of ideas that flowed from it expanded with it.

At that stage, ideas were growing wild, like wild plants; but the time came (as had happened with other wild plants) when it was realized that it paid to cultivate them. Large resources were then turned into 'research and development' with the object of finding new, economically productive, techniques. In capitalist countries the profit motive applied; and socialist countries were not slow to follow the example. The effect of this change in direction has, in the last thirty years, been spectacular. It has given what might be described as a second-order Impulse, an impulse to breed Impulses. Yet, when we look at it in that light, we are bound to contemplate the possibility of its exhaustion. Even a second-order Impulse is an impulse like other Impulses; like other Impulses, may it not peter out?

There are some signs that it may; and some reasons why it may. The consumption goods, which we ordinarily think of as the end-products of the productive process, are themselves means to an end, or ends—the satisfaction of basic human wants. There are not very many of these—food, clothing, housing, and (in a rich society) entertainment. (Entertainment which may be of low, or very high, cultural value.) The wants of most people for these things are very far from being fully satisfied. But it is easier to see those wants being satisfied by an extension of production, by the stretching out of old Impulses (prolonged, as this implies, by induced invention directed to overcoming scarcities) than by the starting of altogether new Impulses—the invention, for instance, of altogether new consumption goods. Seen in this light, the contribution of organized research and development to the satisfaction of basic wants seems, in relation to its cost, rather doubtfully proportionate. Should we not therefore do well to keep open in our minds the possibility that what we have been experiencing is a boom—an exceptional Impulse, which will ultimately relapse into something more moderate—instead of taking it for granted that it must go on for ever.

(2) Economies of scale

I have already distinguished between the two kinds of economies of scale. There is the Adam Smith kind, the specialization of labour; and the characteristically industrial kind, the large plant, the large 'machine'. Each, in formal terms, gives the same advantage, one man devoting his whole time to pin-making (or to car-repairing) produces more than do forty men, each devoting one-fortieth of his time to it; the plant which cost forty times as much produces more than forty times the output. But the optimum size, in the former case, cannot be greater than the whole time of one man; in the latter it is vastly larger.

It may be fully accepted that the latter economy is a major

element in industrial productivity; the economies that are today to be associated with size of plant extend to a point that was undreamed of by Adam Smith. Yet the fact that these latter economies are different in kind, as well as in extent, from the former is of major importance. Specialization of labour increases human skills; and it is a good rule that the more skilled a person is, the more satisfaction he is likely to get from his work. The large scale of industrial production, being dictated by non-human factors, has no such tendency. It does indeed require a very high level of skill from some people; but from most of those who work the machines it makes no such demands. The 'semi-skilled' worker in industry is often less skilled—in the sense that he has to meet fewer calls upon his capacity—than the agricultural labourer. Growth in production, attained in that way, is dearly bought in terms of human happiness. We need look no further to find one of the main causes of industrial unrest.

Add to this the other well-known consequence of the elephantiasis of the machine—monopoly. This first appeared in the form of the monopoly power of large corporations, directed against the consumer or (in various forms of industrial strife) against each other. There were obvious ways of dealing with that—by public ownership, or by public control. But these, we have learnt from bitter experience, are no more than surface remedies; they do not affect the concentration of power. Those who work the great 'machines'—the electricity grid and telephone network are leading examples—have power in their hands. It is much the same power, whether exercised by managers, or by technicians or by (unionized) labour.

There was a stage in the history of industrialism when the large machine, involving large capital investment, was found to give a much improved opportunity for labour to bring pressure upon employers, since the profits that would be lost by interruption of work had become much more considerable. At that stage the large machine was a major factor, perhaps the key factor, in the growth of trade unionism. Its struggle could then be presented as a class war, a struggle of labour against capital. Now, whether under socialism, or under what is left of capitalism, labour and capital are on the same side; labour and technocrats are on the same side; but the struggle persists, as a sectional struggle of each industry against the rest. It is not just a struggle for a fair share in the social product; its effects go deeper even than that. Technical progress itself is threatened, or twisted. Instead of being directed to the increase of production in general, it is directed to the sectional advantage of those engaged in each single industry. It is inevitable that technical progress, when so biased, must be slowed up.

If this is, as some say, the 'English sickness', it is a sickness which other countries appear to be catching. But when we look at the issue in this manner, we may discern a hope—admittedly a faint one—that the two defects of large-scale industrial production which I have been describing may in future to some extent offset one another. If technical changes, devised in the interests of those employed in single industries, should nevertheless be directed towards raising the levels of skill required in those industries, towards improving the quality of work and the conditions of work, so much would be gained that 'monopoly losses' might be a cheap price to pay. It would indeed be a new kind of industrialism; but perhaps there are some faint signs that we are moving towards it.

(3) Land

I shall say very little about the general question of the scarcity of natural resources, since this is a topic which, long forgotten or wished out of sight, is now being discussed so widely by others. This is very natural, in view of current shortages—which, it will be remembered, had become acute at least a year before their aggravation in 1974. Exponential growth is going out of fashion; some economists are even beginning to concern themselves with the problem of reducing the Western world to a stationary state.[8] The shortage of land has come back with a vengeance.

The general shortage of materials is serious; but most particular shortages affect no more than a limited number of industries. The most serious shortage of all, for industrialism, is shortage of power. Already, at the height of the Coal Age, Jevons[9] was predicting the exhaustion of coal supplies; not that the coal would give out, but that it would become harder to get—as it has. Oil came to the rescue; but coal and oil share the common characteristic that their sources are localized, so that their providers, if they get together, can hold the world to ransom. Thus not only the large machine, but also the localization of power supplies, expose industrialism to this sort of challenge.

Such challenges, whether natural or artificial, may in the end be overcome. Induced invention can come to the rescue. But whether directed towards economizing in power, or to the discovery of substitutes, it will have to work very hard—much harder than it seemed to have to work in the time of plenty.

(4) Labour

Hitherto we have been discussing labour in general without making much distinction between kinds of labour. Something must now be said about the distribution of labour between occupations, and about the larger question of distribution between countries.

The theory of the Impulse can be applied in two ways—to a particular country, or to the world as a whole. The former, in the way we are in the habit of thinking, and in the way our facts are presented to us, is the more natural; but if we are to use the theory in that way, it needs some amendment. We must allow for the particular country's external relations.

[8] R.V. Ayres and A.V. Kneese, 'Economic and Ecological Effects of a Stationary Economy' (*Annual Review of Ecology and Systematics*, 1971) is a particularly distinguished example.
[9] W.S. Jevons, *The Coal Question* (1865).

Ideas may come in from abroad; capital, in the sense of saving, may come from abroad or may itself go abroad; natural scarcities may reveal themselves, not directly by what happens within the country, but by a movement of its terms of trade. But what I now want to emphasize in relation to the particular country application is something different. It concerns the process by which real wages rise. I have represented this as a matter of labour scarcity; but we should look at it more closely. Take for the moment the case of an 'advanced' country, one of those in which there has been beyond question a great rise in real wages. Can we attribute that rise to labour scarcity, when it has not (as on the whole it has not) been attended by zero unemployment? When we remember that labour is not homogeneous, I think we can.

We can see, in the first place, that a general expansion must be attended by *particular* labour shortages; some kinds of labour, at least, will prove to be in short supply. Their wages will rise, by the operation of market forces, very strong market forces; for in capitalist countries, unionized or non-unionized, and in socialist countries so long as they give any freedom to the worker, much the same thing happens.

But this is not the end. For there are two ways in which the rise in wages gets spread. One is purely economic. Shortages of particular skills can be overcome. They may be overcome by inventing means of economizing in the scarce labour, using cheaper labour instead, or by training other workers to acquire the necessary skills. The demand for labour is thus shifted from one group to another; both the scarcity and the rise in wages are spread. Even though it does not go so far as to absorb the whole labour supply, of whatever sort, a sufficient expansion will lead to a rise in most wages, implying a substantial rise on the average.

Something of this kind can often, perhaps usually, be traced; but it is not the only way in which spreading occurs. In addition to this economic spreading, there is what we may call social spreading. There are social forces, directed against the upsetting of established differentials (much reinforced by trade unionism, but by no means dependent upon it) which cause the initial, sectional, rise to be spread. 'We are giving more to these people, so we shall have to give more to the others also.' It works like that within the single business; and in a country with some degree of social unity it works to some extent even more widely. This is another reason why the whole labour market does not have to be 'tight'—it is enough that some large parts of it are 'tight'—for there to be a fairly general rise in wages.

I fully grant (to my fellow-economists) that such 'social' spreading is not economically optimum; but economic spreading, as it occurs in practice, itself falls far short of satisfying economic criteria. If the labour market worked like a commodity market, with wages responding directly and quickly to the pressures of supply and demand, what would follow? There might, possibly, be less unemployment; but the ups *and downs* of particular wages would be bound to be considerable. The wages that rose in the initial shortage would have to come down when the shortage was relieved—not indeed to where they were originally, but to a lower level than they had reached at the peak. The fall would of course be resisted. Efforts would be made, and would be attended with some success, to make the temporary advantage permanent.

These things do happen; but it makes for social order that they should not happen too often. So there is something to be said for some degree of social spreading. But it is necessary for social spreading, or for any wide extension of it, that the country should possess some degree of social unity, that most people should regard their fellows as having some at least of the same rights as themselves. It is not much; but in the countries of the world, as at present defined, even this is by no means universal. And almost everywhere it is under threat; from inflation, which brings too much supply and demand into the labour market, setting group against group in a desperate endeavour to defend what they think to be due to them, and from the preachers of discord, for whom these divisions are fair game.

That, however, is not the note on which to conclude. I would rather look up from the case of the single country to the world as a whole. In the world economy, as contrasted with the single country, the sense of social unity is almost entirely lacking. All we have in the way of social spreading are the operations of international bodies, and the grants that are given as aid. In relation to the size of the task, they do not amount to much. But why is more not done by economic spreading? That is the question to which I finally turn.

Let us look at it in the light of the things listed above. We shall find that there is a part of the explanation under each head. Others, no doubt, could usefully be brought in, but let us see how far our four heads will take us.

First, then, let us consider technology. It is not difficult to see why it is in the advanced countries that the main advances in technology are made. So it is from them that the spreading has to occur. Since theirs is the setting in which the advance is made, it is biased towards their needs, rather than towards those of others. Besides, the sheer speed of technical developments causes savings to be diverted towards the exploitation of new opportunities at the expense of the further exploitation of old ones; yet it is the latter which (one would think) would be more to the advantage of the 'under-developed world'. A slowing-down of the boom in technology might, from this point of view, be a help.

Secondly, economies of scale. This is an even more obvious way in which the advanced countries have an advantage. It is hard to achieve great economies in cost unless one can achieve a large size of output; but one cannot *begin* with a large size. Although one may protect an 'infant industry', even the whole of a protected home market is often insufficient for competitiveness. And how often does a protected industry fail to achieve the economies of which, on paper, it ought to be capable! If it should happen that in future industry becomes less dependent on large-scale economies, this barrier would be reduced; so far, however, it has probably been rising.

Thirdly, land. The countries of the world are very unequally provided with natural resources. Some have reliable rainfall, others do not; some sit on mineral deposits, others do not. There were great inequalities, in the days before industrialism, for this reason alone. There are still great inequalities between non-industrialized and lightly industrialized countries, for this reason alone. Some have become rich because of their ample provision with natural resources; they can industrialize if they choose, even though other things are against them, and often they will do so for political rather than economic reasons. It is the others, less well provided, who do not have the wherewithal with which to begin.[10]

Finally, labour. Part of the trouble, surely, is that the strains which, as we have seen, arise in *economic* spreading within the single country, repeat themselves, with even greater intensity, upon the world scale. We have seen how pure economic forces, untempered in their working by social considerations, will almost inevitably cause shortages of particular kinds of labour, and relative rises in the wages of those kinds of labour, but that these advantages will be threatened as time goes on; they will begin to be eroded by the competition of other groups. We have seen that those who are so threatened will look for means of defence. They will defend themselves by trade union action and by various pressures upon their national government. When we project the same issue on the world scale, it is the labour of the advanced countries, as a whole, which is in the threatened position. Although the threat is not so severe, because of the handicaps (some of which I have been listing) imposed upon the potential competitors, the power of resistance exercised through the nation-state is much greater. For while within the nation the pressure of one group may be counterbalanced by pressure from another, a national government, with all that is at its command, cannot resist a pressure that is exercised by its people as a whole.

[10] See my *Essays in World Economics* (1969), pp. 265-9.

I am anxious not to suggest that this last reason (a neo-Marxist one, I suppose it might be called) is the principal cause of retarded development. One has only to point to the case of Japan to show that in favourable circumstances it can be overcome. The others which I have been listing (and others, such as population, which are mentioned earlier in this paper) are in my view more deep-rooted. It is one of the things which must not be forgotten, but no more.

I have found myself trespassing, in these last paragraphs, on matters that are only marginally within the province of the economist. Although I have tried to keep my eyes on the long view, I have inevitably been influenced to some extent by the special problems of the time in which we are living. The strike, which began as a purely economic confrontation between workers and employers, has a different complexion when it is directed, as many now are, against government, against one's own government. And a different complexion again when it is directed against other governments, in pursuit of gains which may be economic, but may be quite non-economic. This, however, is not the place in which to consider these things further. I would only like to conclude by pointing out that it is the development of industrialism which has made them possible.

III MONETARY EXPERIENCE
AND THE THEORY OF MONEY

'Monetary theory', I have observed on another occasion,[1] 'is less abstract than most economic theory; it cannot avoid a relation to reality, which in other economic theory is sometimes missing. It belongs to monetary history, in a way that economic theory does not always belong to economic history. . . . A large part of the best work on Money is topical . . . prompted by particular episodes, by particular experiences of the writer's own time.' I took Ricardo, his concern with monetary reconstruction after the War with Napoleon; and Keynes, his concern with the parallel problem of monetary reconstruction in the 1920s, and then with the Depression of the 1930s, as examples.

I might have added Wicksell, who clearly thought out his monetary theory in relation to the fall in prices in the 1880s and 1890s—a fall is prices which is unmistakable, though we must never forget that evidence about prices was much less good in Wicksell's time than it had become by the time of Keynes. In spite of the relation that undoubtedly exists between Wicksell's monetary theory and his rather formal 'real' or non-monetary theory, he makes it evident that it was this rather long period of falling prices which was the practical issue he had in mind.[2]

Thus we can name three great economists, whose work on Money is pre-eminently important—representing, perhaps, the

---

[1] *Critical Essays in Monetary Theory* (1967), p. 156.

[2] See in particular, his paper *The Influence of the Rate of Interest on Commodity Prices* (1898), English translation in the collection of Wicksell's *Selected Papers on Economic Theory* (1958), pp. 67–89. There is a discussion of Wicksell's work in its historical context in J.R.T. Hughes, 'Wicksell on the Facts' (in *Value, Capital and Growth*, ed. J.N. Wolfe, 1968, pp. 215–55).

three major turning-points in the history of monetary theory—
each of whom was prompted to develop his ideas by a question which had come up in the world at the time when he was
writing. In each case it was a new question; the experience
which raised it was different from anything which had been
experienced before. It is true that both Ricardo's problem
and Keynes's (in the twenties) were problems of post-war
reconstruction; but they were very different problems, all
the same. And it is true that both Wicksell's problem and
Keynes's (in the thirties) were problems of Depression; but
again they were different problems, raising different (theoretical) questions. Each of the theoretical turning-points which I
have been listing can thus be regarded as a response to a *new*
stimulus.

We, in our day, have had a new experience, a new monetary
experience, which could give a comparable stimulus. Prices, in
nearly all countries, after creeping upwards in the fifties and
sixties, have since 1970 shot up much more violently. I think
not merely of the (perhaps pathological) case of Britain, where
the consumer-price index had already doubled (on a base of
1970) by the end of 1975. Much more 'stable' countries have
also seen a large rise. The comparable figure for Germany is
nearly 40 per cent up; that for the United States nearly 50
per cent; for France 60 per cent; for Japan 80 per cent. These
are rises at a rate that had never occurred before, in 'stable'
countries, excepting in war-time. And (what on most previous
experience would seem almost unbelievable) they have been
accompanied by high rates of unemployment, and threats of
even greater unemployment. This is a new phenomenon, a
startling new phenomenon.

It is such that one might expect it to give a stimulus, like
that to which Ricardo, and Wicksell, and Keynes, responded.
It has of course led to mountains of discussion. But it has
not, so far, engendered a New Theory. Most of those who
take part in these discussions have just been going back to the
old theories (even the Keynes theory, by now, is an old
theory), trying to see the new experience through spectacles

that were made for the old. Doubtless there is much to be learned from the old theories; but if we are to use them to best advantage we must see them for what they are.

I make no pretence that in what follows I shall be constructing a New Theory; perhaps I can take a few steps towards it, but no more. I shall still, for the most part, be going back to the old theories; but I shall look at them in the light of the experience which led to them, contrasting it with ours. This does seem to bring out some points which could be useful, and of which, in a final section, I shall try to make use.

The first of them is simple, but far-reaching. Almost universally, and almost throughout history, money has been a national institution (or state institution); money is a means of paying debts, debts which are recognized in particular legal systems, systems which derive their authority from particular states. It is inevitable, in view of this, that most discussions of monetary problems should relate to the moneys of particular countries; so it has been throughout, and so it is today. But when we look at the work of those great monetary economists whom I have been listing, we find that a great part of it is not of this character.

Ricardo, indeed, was mainly concerned with national money; the reconstruction of the British monetary system was his chief concern. But Wicksell's problem (the fall in prices in the eighties and nineties) was an international problem; and so was the Depression of the 1930s, which had a similar relation to the *General Theory* of Keynes. Each of them, therefore, was thinking in world terms. Each of them, therefore, unlike the general run of monetary writers, was content to work with a model that was *closed*. The model was closed, because the world is closed.

It may indeed be admitted that they had other reasons for working with a closed model. It had long been the practice of economists, in non-monetary theory, to do most of their work with a closed model, leaving 'international trade' for separate discussion. To some extent it still is. That very likely explains why the closed-economy model turned out to be fruitful. It cannot do the whole job, but it is a good way to start. That may well hold, even today.

It may hold, for that reason, but for the more practical reason too. The inflation of the 1970s, like the Depression of the thirties, and like the falling prices of the 1880s and 1890s, is a world problem. It affects different countries differently, but so did they. So for this reason too, it may be wise to begin with a 'closed economy' approach.

We in our case may indeed find it more difficult to do so. When Wicksell was writing, rates of exchange between major currencies were fairly stable; so to think of money as inter-national money—in substance, though not in form, a world currency—was fairly natural. It was certainly less natural when Keynes was writing; the changes in exchange rates which had occurred during the Great Depression had been an important part of its story. (Notice, however, that by 1935 the pound-dollar exchange rate had returned, almost exactly, to its old parity; other currencies also appeared to be about to fall into line.) However exchanges 'floated' in the thirties, large changes were still regarded as exceptional. There was none of the floating *on principle* which we have experienced since 1971.

One may therefore admit that we cannot proceed, now, without more attention to the 'nationalization' of money than was necessary in former times. But this does not mean that it may not still be useful to begin with a closed economy. After all, as has been insisted, our problem is a world problem.

I therefore propose, in the greater part of this paper, to follow Wicksell, and the Keynes of the *General Theory*, con-sidering the theory of Money in a closed economy. That, however, raises a further question.

We need to go back before Wicksell, to the days when the Quantity theory of Money reigned supreme. In view of the modern revival of the Quantity theory, that is unavoidable; we have to show how it fits in. We have to begin with the Quantity theory of Money in a closed economy. Ricardo, there, is not much help to us. Though he did have a theory of the 'world' value of money, explaining it in terms of the real cost of production of the money metal, it was a very long-run theory, an almost incredibly long-run theory, so long-run as to be uninformative. It was not in this direction that he made his mark on monetary thinking. So it is better to go back before Ricardo, to the fountain-head of 'classical' monetary theory, the *Essay on Money* of David Hume (1752).

Hume, it must be admitted, is not a good example of topicality; the current events which prompted him to write are not at all obvious.[3] He did nevertheless have practical problems, and examples, in mind. For the case of an increase in 'hard' money in a closed system—the case where a simple Quantity theory effect is least disputable—he had only one major example, and it was not a recent example, though it was a story which was emphasized in the history books which he used. This was the influx of silver from the Spanish possessions in America, between 1560 and 1650, and the rise in prices which was generally associated with it.[4] Without following Hume closely, and without too much attention to this particular historical example, it will be useful to be thinking of this kind of case while we survey, very briefly, the Classical Quantity theory.

One point, however, from the practical example we may

[3] It is indeed an interesting question what led him to write that essay. He was a professional philosopher, turning over to history; his economic essays are a very temporary halting-ground on the way. There is just one piece of evidence which may provide a clue—the long letter which he wrote to Montesquieu at a relevant date (April 1749). It is notable that a considerable proportion of his comments on Montesquieu relate to points which were to come up in the economic essays. So it may well have been the rather undistinguished chapters on economics in the *Esprit des lois* which were the stimulus.

[4] According to Earl Hamilton (*American Treasure and the Price Revolution in Spain*, 1934), the price-level, in Spain, approximately doubled between 1550 and 1600, rising again by another 50 per cent between 1600 and 1650. Even if these figures are taken at their face value, they show a very slow rise in comparison with what we have recently experienced. (It is pointed out by Vicens Vives, *Economic History of Spain* (Princeton, 1969), p. 380, that the rise in prices appears to have begun well in advance of the influx of silver.)

take over. There is no question at all, in this kind of case, that the supply of money is exogenous. Though effects of prices on the incentive to prospect for precious metals have sometimes been traced, it can have no particular (new) shortage of gold and silver that sent Cortes and Pizarro to Mexico and Peru. As far as economic incentives are concerned, they might have gone at any time. Here, then, there is no doubt that the influx of silver is the cause, whatever may have been its effects.

(i) The Classical Quantity Theory

The crudest form of Quantity theory (not, even today, entirely extinct) makes the level of *prices* depend upon the Quantity of money; but the Classical theory, if we take it in the form which Hume (already) gave to it, was not so crude as that. The initial effect of an increase in the supply of money, Hume was aware, is to stimulate industry; 'it must first quicken the diligence of every individual before it increase the price of labour'.[5] A possible effect on output, as well as on prices, must therefore be allowed for. When both are looked at together, it is the total value of output (PQ as we shall write it) which must be supposed to be dependent upon the supply of money (M). It is the Classical theory in that sense (or that part of the Classical theory) with which we shall in this section be mainly concerned.

M is a stock and PQ is a flow; a bridge between them has got to be found. It is found no more than formally if we just introduce V, a 'velocity'; to put $MV = PQ$ does no more than define a ratio; mere definition has no explanatory power. It has to be implied that the ratio (V) is in practice stable; but why should it be? Any regularities that are found in practice themselves require to be explained.

There is a simple model, from which (one suspects) the term 'velocity of circulation' is itself derived, where the explanation is obvious. It is nevertheless, when one looks at it

[5] Hume, *Essays* (Oxford University Press), p. 294.

closely, quite a peculiar model; but it will serve us as a basis from which to begin.

Consider an economy which uses metallic money as its means of payment but which in other respects is financially quite undeveloped. Borrowing and lending need not be entirely absent, but loans are very difficult to arrange. Nearly everyone, therefore, is obliged to limit his spending in any period to what he receives in that period, except in so far as he can make use of savings which he himself has made in the past. These savings, if they are to be used for current expenditure, will have to be held in money form. Thus he can swing about from saving to dis-saving, but he cannot dis-save unless he has already saved. It might be expected that in such an economy there would be a bias in favour of saving, or non-spending, since in the absence of borrowing facilities, the advantages of having a reserve, to meet emergencies, would be very great. That however must for the present be neglected (I shall come to it later). In the model all money received from sales is handed on in purchases (after a lag). It will do no harm to the argument if we assume the lag to be uniform; let us call it one *period*.

If the supply of money increases (by the exploitation of a new source of supply, as in the Spanish case), the effect in such a model is evident. The silver, we may call it, comes in the first place into the hands of its producers, and perhaps into the hands of a king, to whom taxes are paid. It has no further effect until it is spent, but after the lag it will be spent. Demands, in money terms, for non-money commodities will accordingly increase. The sellers of these commodities will then find their receipts increased, so they have more to spend. As they spend their gains, there will be a secondary expansion; and as the gains from that are spent, there will be a third. There will thus be a triangular expansion, as shown in the following table.

We start at the point when the new silver first appears; and we suppose that its output, from then on, is at a steady rate, m per *period*. Then, if we label the recipients of the successive money gains I, II, III, IV . . . (these groups will no doubt over-lap) the additional 'incomes', due to the new money, will be as shown.

The first column, marked 0, shows outputs of silver. Period 1 is the period in which the new silver is first produced, yielding income to its producers, but is not yet spent. In period 2, the silver produced in period 1 is spent on products of I. In period 3, the gain from that is spent on products of II, while the value of I output is kept up by the spending of the silver produced in period 2. And so on.

	0	I	II	III	IV
1	m	-	-	-	-
2	m	m	-	-	-
3	m	m	m	-	-
4	m	m	m	m	-
5	m	m	m	m	m

It will be seen that the income generated, in period 5, is $5m$ (m from production of new silver, and $4m$ from the spending of what has been formerly produced). And this is equal to the new money produced, since the start of the process, as shown in column 0. But this does not mean that new money just generates income equal to itself; we get this effect in our table because we are working in terms of circulation periods.

Suppose that in a year there are h circulation periods. h does not need to be a whole number, so we may round off a little. The total income generated during the first year (by the formula for the area of a triangle) will be $\frac{1}{2} m h^2$. Now $\frac{1}{2} m h$ is the new money that has been produced by the *middle* of the year. So if this is taken as representative of the stock of new money *over* the year, we have

income generated $= h \times$ stock of new money

so the velocity of circulation equals h, as it should.

The same can readily be shown to hold for subsequent years. The income generated, in first and second years together, is $\frac{1}{2} m (2h)^2$; so that which is generated in the second

second year is $\frac{1}{2} m [(2h)^2 - h^2] = (3/2) m h^2$.

$(3/2) mh$ is the new money produced by the middle of the second year; so again

income generated $= h \times$ stock of new money.

And so on, for subsequent years. The velocity of circulation is constant.

All this may seem very obvious, but it has been useful to work it out, if only to contrast it with what happens when we leave these elementary assumptions. The next step is to suppose that (with borrowing and lending still absent) there is a bias in favour of saving. There may still be some spending out of 'hoards', but the advantages of having a reserve are such that more goes in than comes out. This can be formally represented by supposing that, instead of all money received being handed on (after a lag), no more than a proportion c is handed on, the remainder being saved—and there is still no way of holding savings excepting in money form. Here then at (say) the fifth circulation period, while the increase in money stock is still $5m$, as before, the income generated is no more than

$$m (1 + c + c^2 + c^3 + c^4),$$

which is less than $5m$. In 'velocity of circulation' terms, velocity continually diminishes, as more and more of the new money disappears into hoards. As time goes on, the money stock still increases indefinitely; but the income generated does not increase indefinitely. It is always less than a fixed limit.[6]

[6] In order to round off as before, we must put $e^{-\gamma}$ for c. Then income generated in circulation period N is

$$m \int_0^N e^{-\gamma t} dt = (m/\gamma) (1 - e^{-\gamma N}).$$

Income generated in the year from $N = nh$ to $N = (n + 1) h$ is

$$\int_{nh}^{(n + 1)h} (m/\gamma) (1 - e^{-\gamma t}) dt$$
$$= (m/\gamma) [h - (1/\gamma) e^{-\gamma nh} (1 - e^{-\gamma h})].$$

The limit of this when γ tends to O is m h^2 (n + $\frac{1}{2}$), consistently with what was found for the "non-hoarding" case; but if γ is not zero, it is always less than (mh/γ). When γ is small, this limit may be quite large; but it does *not* increase with n.

There is thus a 'leak' in the monetary system, the leak which has often been suspected by 'currency cranks'. It is not in itself to be denied. The use of money does provide an opportunity for saving, but it does not, in itself, provide an opportunity for the savings to be used. It is, however, the lack of financial development which is responsible for the 'leak'. As soon as borrowing and lending are permitted, it can readily be offset.

This is so, even while we keep to the assumption that metallic money is the only means of payment. For it is now no longer the case that spending in excess of receipts can only be financed from one's own past savings; it now becomes possible to spend in excess, by borrowing the difference from someone else. Since the lender is to accept the borrower's promise to repay in place of the money which he is handing over (and this promise cannot be used for expenditure in emergencies, directly, as a 'hoard' of money could be), he will require a payment of interest in compensation for the liquidity that he is giving up. (How much liquidity is given up depends in part on the terms of the loan, and in part upon the extent of facilities for selling his claim to someone else; that is to say, upon the extent of development of a capital market.) The payment of interest is indeed an incentive to saving; but interest will not be promised if the borrowed funds[7] are intended to be idle.

So consider the effect of new money in a system where such opportunities are present. Both the producers of the new money, and those on whose products the new money is spent, will not simply find their incomes rising; at the same time their credit is improved, so that they will find it easier to borrow. Some of them, at least, will want to borrow, so that spending will increase *more* rapidly than it did in our first model.[8]

---

[7] It will be noticed that in this model idle money does not itself carry interest. See below, pp. 62–3.

[8] Bearing in mind Hume's insistence that the initial expansion is a *real* expansion, not a mere rise in prices, it is not unreasonable to expect that it will lead to a desire for increased investment, on the conventional "accelerator" lines.

So there is no 'leak'—rather the opposite.

But just as a tendency to spend less than receipts implied a piling-up of hoards, so a tendency to spend more implies a running-down. So the system cannot continue indefinitely upon an 'excess-expansionary' path without feeling a strain. The funds that are needed to support the excess expansion must become harder to get. As a symptom of this rates of interest are likely to rise; but shortage of funds cannot be remedied, indefinitely, by higher interest rates. The shortage itself is bound to set a limit. There must be a ceiling.

If the expansion has been sharp, and the encounter with the ceiling is sharp, there will be a crisis—the essence of which is that the liquidity of loans, previously made, is called in doubt. Those who have made the loans will thus find their capital diminished; so that not only will they be less willing to make further loans, but they will be seeking to add to the part of their capital which they hold in money form. Spending thus diminishes sharply; the system reverts, for the moment, to the 'excess-saving' condition that we previously considered.

Must the fall, nevertheless, encounter a floor? As is usually the case with fluctuations, it is harder to demonstrate the necessity of a floor than to demonstrate the necessity of a ceiling. But consider the extreme case, the very extreme case, in which *all* the loans that were made during the preceding boom have suddenly become worthless. Even then there remains the (temporarily unchanged) supply of metallic money, and it would be absurd to suppose that all of it would be in the hands of those who would want to hoard it. Thus even then spending would continue, though at a low level; in less extreme cases, when there is much of the economy that has not participated in the boom, and when the shock has been less violent, the floor may not be so low. New borrowers, and new lenders, can then arise; so, after a time, there will be a recovery.[9]

---

[9] Recovery will of course be easier if there is an underlying expansion, going on all the time, in the (metallic) money supply.

I have thought it worth while to trace out this 'cycle', at least so far, for two reasons. On the one hand, it demonstrates the possibility of fluctuations—monetary fluctuations—in an economy which has no bank money or other paper money (as we are still assuming). It is the presence of a capital market which is the condition for them, not the presence of banking. The other reason is that it gives the Quantity theory itself a new look. The fluctuations that are possible, in such an economy, are fluctuations about an *equilibrium path*, as shown in Fig. 1. It is fair to suppose that along that path, where there is neither excess saving nor excess dis-saving, income generated will be proportional to the supply of money; for along that path there is neither hoarding nor dishoarding—money is simply circulating in a normal manner. But the economy does not have to stick to that path; it is simply that the extent to which it can diverge from that path is limited.[10]

[10] It is interesting to find that some of the symptoms of a "cycle", such as has been described, can already be distinguished in the story of the Spanish silver, which has been kept in mind in the foregoing. These events preceded the general rise in banking; but a capital market did exist, though it must have been quite rudimentary.

The King of Spain (Philip II), who was the chief direct recipient of the new silver, did not confine himself to spending what he got from it, but borrowed on the strength of his future receipts. He had in fact a strong incentive to do so, since his most important source of "ordinary" tax revenue, the Low Countries (Holland and Belgium to be), was threatened, just at the time when the supply of silver accelerated (about 1560), by religious unrest. His reign was accordingly punctuated by financial crises, of grave political importance. The first point at which he found himself unable to pay his armies, which were keeping order in the Netherlands, because he was unable to borrow further, was in 1575; the result was an army mutiny (the "Spanish fury") which led to the first overt Netherlandish revolt. That was a major disaster, but from it, as we should expect, there was a recovery. The silver continued to come in; so, after a time, liquidity was restored. But then in due time it all happened again. The second crisis (in 1596) stopped his most promising attempt to recover control in the Netherlands, and (as it turned out) set the seal on Dutch independence.

Some details about these borrowings are given in Vicens Vives, op. cit., pp. 348–51.

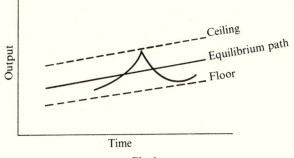

Fig. 1.

It may well be that as long as we keep to our metallic money assumption, that metallic money is the only means of payment, the extent of divergence from the equilibrium path that can occur must be very limited; but that is a hard matter to test, for the rise of the capital market and the rise of banking are developments that historically went together, and perhaps had to go together. With generalized borrowing and lending the metallic money assumption is hard to maintain. If it is taken strictly, it implies that all transactions are 'spot' transactions—money passing one way and goods (or services) the other, contemporaneously. Even at a low level of financial development, that can hardly hold without exception. One of the earliest ways of spending in excess of receipts is by issuing promises to pay. If goods are delivered now, but payment is only made later, are we to say that the goods have not been sold until they have been paid for? It is not common practice to do so; yet if we do not do so we must admit that the promise to pay has become (if only temporarily) a kind of money.

That just becomes more formal with the rise of banking. This builds upon the base of the metallic money a pyramid of money substitutes; they gradually become firmer, until finally the transfer of a banker's promise to pay is regarded as closing a transaction. It is unnecessary to go into detail, distinguishing, for instance, between notes and deposits; we may proceed directly to the consideration of a developed banking system, such as existed (more or less) at the end of the nineteenth century, where a primary metallic money (now—realistically— gold) is still in general use, though a substantial superstructure of bank credit has been built upon it.

We are to look, as has been insisted, at the international system, now the system of the regular Gold Standard. It could be represented, at this date, by a model consisting of a group of countries, each with its own banking organization, which is issuing a national bank money. The national currencies are, however, kept convertible, at approximately fixed parities, into the money metal. Realistically, there would have been countries outside this system, but in the model they may be disregarded.

It is of the greatest importance that a system of this kind could be looked at it in two (or perhaps even three) quite different ways. That which is nearest to the approach which we have been elaborating would insist on regarding the gold base as *the* money, the rest being just money substitutes, which enable the gold base to support a larger value of output, just as the loans had done in the model previously considered. If one was prepared to look on the Gold Standard in this way, the Quantity theory, in the form it has here been taken, would not need to be greatly changed. There would still be an Equilibrium path, along which the value of output would be determined by the supply of gold, as it was by the supply of silver in our previous example.

There would indeed, as already indicated, be possibilities of fluctuation; sometimes the available gold would be fully used, sometimes much less fully used. And if no more is said than this, the possibilities of fluctuation would seem to be very large. If the value of output rose above its Equilibrium path, there would indeed be a strain on the gold supply; the bankers, in particular, would find themselves, in the end, over-extended. Thus, as before, there would be a ceiling; and for much the same reasons it is intelligible that there would be a floor. The cycles that would be generated in this way agree fairly well with those that are in fact recorded. They would carry with them fluctuations in prices. But the independence of the gold base would keep the fluctuations within limits (though they might be wide limits); so they would be felt as fluctuations about a normal level. In the depressions prices would be felt to be low, in the booms to be high. The normal level itself would change rather slowly, with changes in productivity (and hence in the supply of goods) and with changes in the supply of gold—from the mines.

So far as the Gold Standard period is concerned, this does not fit the facts at all badly. There were fluctuations, as expected; the longer period trends, which appear to be observable, seem also to be explained. If prices were tending to fall, between 1875 and 1895, that is what we should on this view expect. Productivity was increasing quite rapidly, but the output of gold was rather sluggish. The change in the price trend, which begins to be observable in the middle nineties, and is unmistakable after 1900, matches the new gold, coming in from the Rand. So there was no necessary reason, so far, to abandon a Quantity theory—if that is qualified in the way we have seen reason to qualify it.

It could nevertheless be questioned, already, if that was enough. Gold, in some important 'member' countries, was already passing out of private circulation; it was becoming a specialized money, used by banks in settling accounts with one another, but much less used outside the banking system. So, it could well be maintained, the time had come to turn over to regarding the bank money as being *the* money; if the Quantity theory was to be maintained, it was to the Quantity of bank money that it must apply. That is a step which was very generally taken (as by modern monetarists it is still taken); it is nevertheless a serious step, which makes a difference.

There is no question, as we have seen, that when money is a metallic money, its supply can be treated as an exogenous variable; major changes in supply, at least, come in from 'outside'. But the supply of bank money is not so clearly exogenous. It can indeed be affected by changes in banking policy; but with given policy (as represented, more or less, by given lending rates) the supply of bank money is determined by the market. It is provided by the banks, to the extent that the market requires, so it is *not* an exogenous variable. It is true that this may be in practice concealed (or partly concealed) in so far as the banking system works under rules, that have been imposed upon it—rules which maintain some form of attachment between the supply of bank money and an external base (in the Gold Standard period the supply of gold). If the rules were completely firm, the supply of bank money would then be a function of the supply of gold, and of that only—so that the supply of bank money, also, could be regarded as an exogenous variable. That is what a Quantity theory, in these new conditions, must imply; one can in fact see this interpretation at work in the textbooks of the period, which reduce so much of what they have to say about the working of the monetary system to these rules and regulations.[11] It could nevertheless be questioned, even then, whether the rules were as firm as pretended. In a particular country they might be fairly firm; but they were surely quite loose, when the international monetary

[11] I am thinking of the textbooks of the latter part of the century, by which time, at least in Britain, the rules and regulations were becoming codified (Fiduciary issues, reserve ratios, and so on). The great *classical* writings on monetary theory preceded the codification, so they (rightly) were less mechanical. An outstanding example is the chapter on the "Influence of Credit on Prices" in John Stuart Mill's *Principles*, which I think I can claim to be quite in harmony with the version of classical theory presented here.

I shall no doubt be told that my version owes too much to Keynes (especially to the Keynes of the *Treatise*) to be properly representative of *classical* doctrine; but I think that chapter of Mill's is there to prove the contrary. It will be noticed that I have not needed (or hardly needed) to make use of Keynes's concepts of Investment and Saving. One does not have to ask about the use that is made of the funds that are borrowed; Philip II's armies, and nineteenth-century railway-building, are *from the monetary point of view*, all on a par.

system is considered as a whole.

If one was unwilling to lay such stress upon rules and regulations, and if one nevertheless insisted on bank money being *the* money, it would have to be *banking policy*, rather than the supply of money, which would would have to treat as one's exogenous variable. (It could indeed be admitted that banking policy might be affected by the supply of gold, but that would now be taken *outside* the model.) So we come to Wicksell, who was the first to attempt a theory of this new type.

As I have indicated, I am not wholly convinced that at Wicksell's date (*Interest and Prices*, 1898) his new approach was necessary. It may be that it was still sufficient to use a Quantity theory, in one or other of its forms; I would prefer to leave that as an open question. But there is no doubt at all that Wicksell was forward-looking. The monetary system was about to undergo a revolution, which would lead it much further in his direction. That is why he is so important.

(ii) Wicksell

Though he qualified it in application, Wicksell's model is best understood as a pure credit model; there is no money that is not credit. All money is someone's promise to pay; but to pay what? If the promise is not to be nugatory (as the promise that is printed on the British pound note has become nugatory), and if there is no 'hard' money in which payment can be made, all that can be promised is the convertibility of the one promise into another, another promise which the creditor may at the moment prefer.

It must be supposed that promises by different agents have different degrees of reliability; these may well be changing, relatively to one another, from time to time. There will be some which for the moment have greatest reliability. If there was just one agent, the reliability of whose promises was always greater than the reliability of any other's, his promise to pay would indeed be nugatory; and that is indeed a case which is important in the working of national economies, where by act of government the liabilities of a particular institution (its Central Bank) can be made *legal tender*. In the international economy (to which our present discussion refers, and our interpreation of Wicksell refers) it does not arise, for there is no legal tender. Here, however, there is another way out.

We may suppose that there exists a group, or family, of institutions, promises to pay by each of which have maximum reliability, or ordinarily have maximum reliability. The promise to pay by each is a promise to exchange its promise, if required to do so, into a promise issued by another. A is saying 'My promise is as good as B's, but if you don't like my promise, I will arrange for you to have B's'. A group of institutions, maintaining this relation, may be regarded as issuing a pure credit money. We shall describe the group, by which this money is issued, as the Banking System.

The individual banks, which comprise the System, are in competition with one another. The funds which they lend are (for the most part) funds which they themselves have borrowed; and since it is to the interest of each bank to extend its business, it will (subject to considerations of prudence) seek to borrow more, in order to have more to lend. It will seek to attract funds, and must therefore, at least in principle, pay interest on its deposits—on the funds that it borrows. This (as we shall see) has not always been made clear; it would, however, appear to be an essential characteristic of a pure credit model.

A bank's lending rate will have to exceed its borrowing rate, since otherwise the bank could not cover its administrative costs and could make no profit; but in a competitive system, that margin should be quite narrow. A consequence of this is that one assumption that we have hitherto been making no longer holds. We could assume, so long as we were concerned with a metallic money system, in which money does not bear interest, that funds were unlikely to be borrowed unless it was intended that they should be spent. Here that cannot be true. For to borrow from the Banking System, and then to re-deposit with the Banking System, now involves no more than a small sacrifice of interest (just the difference between the bank's lending rate and its borrowing rate); the additional liquidity, gained from being able to call on funds whenever one wants them, may well be worth that modest price.

It is this, more than anything else, which makes the Quantity theory inapplicable to the pure credit economy. The Quantity of Money must now mean the Quantity of bank money; but a substantial part of the Quantity of bank money is now, in principle, idle. So the total Quantity of money may vary considerably, while the part which is not idle is substantially unchanged. The link between the total Quantity of Money and that part of it which circulates is effectively snapped.

A widening of the margin, between the lending rate and the borrowing rate of the Banking System, will indeed reduce the demand for idle money; but it need have no effect upon the demand for money to spend. If the lending rate is raised, while the deposit rate is not raised, this may well be all that happens. But if both rates rise, the margin between them being unchanged, there is a more reliable effect on spending. For not only does the higher lending rate deter borrowing from the Banking System; by the rise in the deposit rate the opportunity cost of spending, from funds that had previously been borrowed for the sake of liquidity, is also increased. On both scores, therefore, the incentive to spend is diminished.

It seems to follow that when one is constructing a simple model of a pure credit system, it is appropriate to neglect the margin between borrowing and lending rates, letting the pair be represented by a single *rate of interest*. It is that rate of interest which becomes the effective monetary regulator, not the Quantity of Money, in any sense.

That, I believe, is what in effect Wicksell did. He began from the regular principle, already accepted fairly generally, that reductions in interest are expansionary, increases contractionary; no one who watched the effect of 'bank rate' (or its equivalents) on markets could doubt that, so far as immediate effects were concerned. There had, however, been doubts about longer-run effects, based partly upon the view that higher interest raised costs and that this must in the end raise prices; but more substantially upon the historical evidence that rates of interest were usually high when prices were rising and low when they were falling. It was, however, not difficult to show how this 'paradox' could arise, consistently with the long-run validity of the regular principle. All that needed to be implied by the principle was that *other things being equal* expansion would be greater (or contraction less) at lower rates of interest than at higher; so no more was shown by the observed movement, over the 'cycle', than that the Banking System was acting, on the whole, as a stabilizer. Falling prices diminished the demand for loans; thus the demand for loans became less than the banking system was willing to provide; the fall in interest was a natural reaction. So far as the cycle was concerned, no more than that was required.[12]

Wicksell, however, was saying much more than that. For, as he himself makes abundantly clear,[13] it was the long-run fall in prices, during the twenty years which preceded his time of writing, not the cyclical fluctuations of much shorter period, which was what he wanted to explain. It did not seem to be explicable by an adaptation of the cyclical argument. It was understandable that in a slump falling prices would choke off investment, and it was understandable that it would take some time for that state of mind to be changed, even by continued monetary ease; but how was one to explain the long-run fall on those lines? In twenty years there was plenty of time.

One could, however, go back to the principle from which the discussion had started. Just why is investment supposed

[12] It will be noticed that such a view, of interest and the cycle, is entirely consistent with a Quantity theory, as we have here expounded it. "Tightness" and "ease" of the money market could still be interpreted in terms of scarcity and plenty of hard money reserves.

[13] See the paper on interest and commodity prices (above, p. 45, p. 68); what is said in the *Lectures* on cyclical fluctuations (see below, p. 68) bears it out.

to become more advantageous when interest is lower? It must be a matter of comparison between the interest charged and the expected return. The latter is partly a question of the relation between the present prices, at which the money borrowed will be spent, and the future prices, at which the resulting product is expected to be sold; it is easy to understand that when prices are falling, this relation will seem less advantageous than it would be if prices were steady. That, however, has already been taken into account. But it is also a matter of the *real* return on investment, the productivity, in terms of real goods, of the inputs on which the borrowed money is to be spent. Wicksell's distinctive contribution, at the next stage of his work (coming after the crucial decision to work with a credit economy), was to emphasize the importance of this real return, the *natural rate of interest* as he called it.

There are many problems about the natural rate of interest; some of them we shall consider later. We shall, however, consider them more usefully, and less abstractly, if we begin by seeing how Wicksell thought he could use it. It was not unreasonable to suppose that real return had been rather lower in the years that were in Wicksell's mind than it had been in the preceding quarter-century; the exhaustion of the best opportunities for railway-building could well have that effect.[14] To Wicksell, this would imply a fall in the natural rate. All that would then be required to explain the falling prices—the falling trend of prices—would be to suppose that the banking system had failed to react sufficiently; it had indeed allowed interest rates to fall, but it had only done so after a lag. That would be enough.

So we come to the central doctrine, what still is *the* Wicksell doctrine. If the actual (or market) rate of interest is below the natural rate, prices will rise; if it is above, prices will fall; so long as the discrepancy persists, the rise (or fall)

[14] See above, p. 17.

will continue indefinitely, or as Wicksell would say 'cumulatively'. It is clear, from what has been said, that the natural rate, of which Wicksell was thinking, was a *real* rate; but how can a real rate, which must be expressed in terms of goods, or of some bundle of goods, be compared with a market rate of interest, which must be expressed in terms of money?

There are several ways out. There is Keynes's way; we may say that what has to be compared with the market rate of interest is not Wicksell's real rate, but the Marginal Efficiency of Capital, itself a money rate, influenced not solely by Wicksell's real factors, but also by price-expectations and, even more generally, by the state of mind of entrepreneurs. We shall come to that; there is something like it which may well find a place in Wicksell's theory; but I feel sure that it was not this which in Wicksell's central doctrine is implied. Nor is it wise to run on, in the manner of Wicksell's successors,[15] converting the Wicksell model into a sophisticated model of equilibrium over time, current investment depending on expectations and equilibrium a condition in which expectations are not disappointed. All these are things which have grown out of the Wicksell model; but when we look at Wicksell in the light of his own problem, his own experience, we shall surely interpret him in a simpler way.

Begin with a state which he would have described as one of equilibrium; a state in which prices are stable, and are expected with confidence so to remain. There is then no question that the real rate of return can be interpreted as a money rate of return; equality between that rate of return and the actual market rate, as a condition of equilibrium, makes sense. If, now, the market rate is reduced below that natural

---

[15] Lindahl, papers published in Swedish in 1929–30, and translated in his *Studies in the Theory of Money and Capital* (1939); Myrdal, in German 1933, translated as *Monetary Equilibrium* (1939). In much of my own work, *Value and Capital* (1939), and *Capital and Growth* (1965), ch. 6, I have followed in their footsteps. But I have since come to feel that when one looks at Wicksell in his historical context, it is not quite right to do so.

rate, bank lending will expand, and prices (in the first place just some prices) will start to rise. But so long as the rise in prices is regarded as temporary, the high prices now, compared with unchanged prices expected later on, would discourage borrowing; a 'pseudo-natural rate' (as we might call it) would develop, which would be lower than the true natural rate; between that and the actual market rate there need be no discrepancy. But if the market rate continued at its lower level, while the natural rate continued at its unchanged level, this could not hold. As time went on, expectations of prices would be revised, upwards. So the pseudo-natural rate would be revised, upwards. If it did no more than return to equality with the true natural rate, the initial discrepancy would be repeated, and prices would rise, again. That could happen again and again—Wicksell's 'cumulative process'.

Even this, however, may be too 'expectational', relying too much upon a difference between current prices and prices which are expected to rule in the future. A later generation of economists would find such an interpretation easy; but to attribute it to Wicksell at his date is probably an anachronism. He himself draws particular attention to the effect of interest-changes on capital good prices; thus a disequilibrium between capital good prices and consumption good prices looks much more like being his answer.

On this line of thought the first effect of the reduced (actual) rate of interest would be an increase in the demand for capital goods (as inputs). There would certainly be some such goods the supply of which could not respond immediately (if indeed it could respond at all[16]) so that some capital good prices at least would surely rise. This price-rise would carry with it windfall gains, some of which would in time be spent; thus the demand for consumption goods would also rise, in time, but not immediately. There would thus be

---

[16] It should be remembered that Wicksell, in his non-monetary theory (as in Volume I of the *Lectures*), was very insistent that "original" inputs included land as well as labour.

an interim, during which input prices have risen, but output prices have not yet risen. During that interim the money return on investment would be diminished, by the relative rise in input prices; so here also there would be a pseudo-natural rate, reduced below the true natural rate, and thus brought back, for the moment, into equilibrium with the actual rate. Nevertheless, as time went on, the demand for consumption goods must increase, and their prices must rise. Thus, as on the other interpretation, the pseudo-natural rate would return towards the true natural rate, and the 'cumulative' expansion would continue.

One could argue in the same way on the other tack. Let us here suppose that it is the natural rate which falls (opportunities for profitable investment at a given rate of interest are diminished), while the actual rate of interest is not reduced. Capital goods prices would fall, thus (for the moment) keeping up apparent profitability. But the fall would also cause windfall losses; these, in their turn, would react on the demand for consumption goods, so, in the end, weakening consumption good prices. So here again the 'cumulative process' would continue.

I do not suppose that Wicksell had any very clear idea of the working of the economy during his 'interim' or 'disequilibrium period'. He had certainly not thought out the effects on employment, to which Keynes was later to devote so much attention. But that a disequilibrium stage played a part in his concept of the 'cumulative process' seems to me undeniable. How else is one to explain his sharp distinction between cycle theory and the longer-run monetary theory which he continually emphasized to be his main concern? In the few pages which he devotes to the cycle (at the end of Volume II of the *Lectures*) he describes conditions in which stocks are changing involuntarily—clearly disequilibrium situations. During the cycle, he emphasizes, the 'natural rate of interest' is very unstable. It is subject to 'erratic shocks' (as Frisch[17] was later

[17] Frisch, *Propagation and Impulse in Dynamic Economics (Essays in honour of Gustav Cassel*, 1933). It will be noticed that Frisch refers to Wicksell.

to call them); the effect of each shock does not have time to work itself out before it is followed by another. But these short-run fluctuations are independent of the *trend*, to which his main argument refers; a trend, such as is represented by the long-run fall in prices between the seventies and the time at which he was writing.[18]

Nevertheless, in terms of that trend, there remains a further issue. As soon as one distinguishes between the movement of one set of prices and that of another set (whether one draws the line between capital good prices and consumption good prices or in any other place) one is faced with the question: what kind of price-stability is it that is to be regarded as consistent with 'equilibrium'? During the twenty years, of which Wicksell was thinking, productivity was rising, rising quite rapidly; labour costs of production were therefore diminishing quite rapidly; should this not mean that it was *proper* for prices, especially consumption good prices, to have a falling trend? One could indeed conceive of an equilibrium in which consumption prices, on the whole, were stabilized, so long as money wages were rising; but would it be any more of an equilibrium than one in which money wages were stabilized, while consumption prices were (appropriately) falling? How does one distinguish between these alternatives, or between the obvious compromises which might be constructed between them, so as to dignify one, rather than another, with the title of equilibrium? There does not appear to be any, within

[18] So the main criticism which I would make of the otherwise admirable study by John Hughes, cited above (a study to which what I am now saying owes a great debt), is that he is not quite following Wicksell when he seeks to apply the actual rate–natural rate doctrine to the slump of 1892–5. It must be implied by what Wicksell says that the lag in interest rates, over the whole period since the seventies, aggravated the depressions, which occurred during that period. But this is a different matter from holding that much could have been done to cure a particular depression by a better interest-rate policy, as Hughes would appear to make Wicksell say.

the Wicksell model, by which one can distinguish.[19]

It must, however, be insisted that in spite of the ambiguity, thus encountered, the central Wicksell doctrine is unchanged. There is now no longer a single natural rate, but a different natural rate for each equilibrium. From the point of view of equilibrium A, the natural rate of equilibrium B is a pseudo-natural rate, which takes account of the movement of prices. If prices are rising more rapidly, or falling less rapidly, in B than in A, the natural rate in B must therefore be higher. But a movement from equilibrium A towards a more rapid price-rise is brought about by a fall in actual interest; thus what is disequilibrium from the point of view of A is an even greater disequilibrium from the point of B. Though we must now recognize that a B-equilibrium is possible, the movement of interest which tends to produce a B-price movement works against the establishment of an equilibrium B.

The doctrine is not changed; but its significance surely is. There is no means of distinguishing between the equilibria, within the Wicksell model; so if we want to distinguish (as we surely must want to distinguish), if we are interested in the prime monetary problems, of inflation and deflation,

---

[19] It is easy for British economists (and historians) who remember that the years of which Wicksell was thinking, the whole twenty years, were regarded by contemporaries as years of Depression, to conclude that over these years there must have been a Wicksellian discrepancy. But this is not at all clearly established by Wicksell's own figures. In the paper, above cited, which is the clearest statement of the practical significance of his theory, as he saw it, he puts on a chart two price-series (index-numbers of wholesale prices, the only price index-numbers then available). One of them is British (the well-known Sauerbeck index), the other German (an index of prices at Hamburg). The German index falls as fast as the British, if anything faster. But these were great years of industrial expansion in Germany; the Germans, at least, do not seem to have been much impeded by their falling prices! Industrial leadership was passing from Britain to Germany (and, of course, to the United States). So relative depression, in British industry, would not seem at all surprising. It is not, in itself, a sign of disequilibrium, in the world economy.

something else must be introduced, from outside. Wicksell himself does not seem to have gone so far as to see that; but Myrdal, in the most important of post-Wicksellian writings,[20] did. He perceived that in the model world, where all prices are equally flexible, there is no means of distinguishing; but in the real world, where some prices (for instance wages) are less flexible, or less responsive, than others, there may be. One equilibrium may then be regarded as 'better' than another if it puts less strain on the less flexible prices, thus enabling the economy to function with smaller excesses, of demand or of supply, in the markets where prices do not equate supply and demand quickly and easily. That, in his view, at the time he was writing (1933), tended to make one favour an equilibrium in which money wages moved little with increasing productivity, while consumer prices, supposed to be flexible, fell. But it is clear that the same principle might tend in different directions in other circumstances.

For the generalization of Wicksell, which we find in Myrdal, cries out to be carried further. We are to select a particular equilibrium (out of the many Wicksellian equilibria now seen to be possible) and to regard it as *the* equilibrium, which against all others is to be preferred. But we can only do this on non-monetary considerations. It can be no more than the course which the economy, in its institutional structure, can most easily follow. Such a course may be one in which prices (as represented by some particular price-index) are constant, or falling, or rising. Monetary considerations alone do not tell us which.

Such an equilibrium, nevertheless, is still an equilibrium, in Wicksell's sense; it can be disturbed by a monetary policy which is inappropriate to it. If the rate of interest is too low to be appropriate, prices will rise, relatively to the course

[20] *Monetary Equilibrium* (above cited). Though Myrdal's book was written and published, in German, before Keynes's *General Theory*, it is interesting to learn that Keynes did not read it until it appeared in English translation, in 1939. (Kahn, 'On re-reading Keynes', *British Academy Proceedings*, 1974.)

which they would have pursued on the equilibrium path; if the rate of interest is too high, they will fall, again relatively. If the discrepancy is maintained there will be an increasing divergence. It is just as in Wicksell, though it looks so different.

Suppose, however, that there is a change in preferences (or in some other external data). The course which has hitherto been pursued (and to which the economy, and its monetary policy, is more or less adjusted) is then found to be intolerable, or untenable. Course has thus to be changed; and let us suppose that the change of direction is to be made by monetary policy. From the point of view of the old equilibrium, any change in monetary policy is disequilibrating; but it is required that a way should be found from that disequilibrium to a new equilibrium. Can that be done by monetary policy alone? It does not, in these terms, look very likely. The establishment of a rate of interest which is appropriate to the new equilibrium will indeed be required, when the new equilibrium is reached; but it must not be established before that equilibrium is reached. It does not look likely that it can be by monetary policy alone that the economy can find its new equilibrium.

These look more like the problems of the 1970s than those of Wicksell's own time. But Wicksell, as we have seen, was very forward-looking.

(iii) Keynes

As Keynes himself recognized, his model is nearer to Wicksell's than to any other with which he was familiar; it will therefore be appropriate, in the present context, to begin our discussion of him by considering just what his essential differences from Wicksell were. Some (the most obvious) we can ascribe to his skill in working with macro-economic aggregates, aggregates which by his time were beginning to be thrown up by the statisticians, so that they were much more readily available to him than they had been to Wicksell; these we may put on one side. There remain some vital differences, which are illuminated when we look at them in relation to the circumstances of the time in which he was writing.

Wicksell's was a theory of Prices, Interest, and Money;[21] Keynes's of Employment, Interest, and Money (as he says). The contrast does not imply, as Keynesians are tempted to think, that Wicksell was unconcerned about the employment of labour. Why should he have been concerned about falling prices, unless it was that he held them to be damaging to the activity of industry, and hence to employment? He *was* concerned about the activity of industry, but in a different way from Keynes.

Wicksell, as we have seen, distinguished sharply between trend and cycle; in Keynes that distinction has disappeared. This is the reason why, in the *General Theory*, he threw over Wicksell's *natural rate*,[22] of which in the *Treatise on Money* he had approved. He does so because he is throwing over Wicksell's long-term equilibrium, an equilibrium which left room for cyclical fluctuations about it; fluctuations which would sometimes reduce employment below its equilibrium level, but sometimes raise it above. In Wicksell's equilibrium there is 'normal employment'. To Keynes, with the Great Depression just behind him, and with nothing, even in the twenties, that looked like normality, 'normal employment' is uninteresting. Full employment, the maximum employment that can be attained by expansion of effective demand, and hence in the money value of output,[23] was the only benchmark that seemed to remain.

This essential change carried with it several others. Long-term equilibrium having disappeared, the way was clear for concentration on the economics of the short period (in what was in effect Marshall's sense). Measures that were taken to

---

[21] *Geldzins und Güterpreise.*

[22] *General Theory*, p. 242.

[23] This is of course different from full employment in the politicians' or administrators' sense; it is grossly unfair to Keynes to mix them up. But his use of so emotive a term invited misunderstanding. 'Involuntary unemployment' did not help.

stimulate demand would not take effect immediately, but they would affect employment in a finite time, and that was as far ahead as (at least in terms of the model) it was necessary to look. So Keynes's *equilibrium* is quite different from Wicksell's; it is just the state in which such short-term forces have had time to work themselves out.

He had still to make a connection between effective demand (most naturally measured in money) and the employment of labour, which is not a monetary magnitude. But we will come to that later. It will be best to begin with the monetary theory of effective demand, where it may still be profitable to consider Keynes's version, contrasting it with Wicksell's version, and with the Classical version, as we can now do. The differences, we shall not now be surprised to find, depend upon the type of monetary system that is being assumed.

We have seen that in the simplest form of monetary system, where all money is hard money and the financial system is undeveloped, there is nothing to be said which cannot be said by some application of the equation of exchange $MV = PQ$. M (the quantity of money) is clearly exogenous; V can be interpreted as a velocity of circulation, determined by habits and institutions, which can also be regarded as among the data of the model. In terms of changes in M on the one hand, and changes in V on the other (lags being allowed for), changes in PQ are here completely explained.

We have also seen that a pure credit system is conceivable, in which the equation of exchange, instead of giving the answer, tells us nothing at all. So at this extreme one comes to Wicksell's determination by rate of interest, the quantity of money dropping out.

In Keynes's model there is a developed financial system; so it should be nearer to the Wicksell model than to the other. Nevertheless he does treat the supply of money (which is evidently to be taken to be bank money) as exogenous. How does he do this? What is the difference between the Keynes model and the Wicksell model which causes them to go different ways on this decisive point?

In the Keynes model money does not bear interest. That is continually emphasized; the simultaneous holding of interest-bearing assets and non-interest-bearing money, in the same balance-sheet, is represented as one of the major things which have to be explained. Now, as we saw when discussing Wicksell, it is in the nature of a *competitive* banking system to offer interest on deposits. Keynes's banking system does not do so; it must therefore be taken to be non-competitive. It is true that non-competitiveness may take quite a number of different forms. It might be, for instance, that it is the banking system as a whole which is non-competitive (one thinks of the 'Cartel' which appears to have operated among the British clearing banks at the time when Keynes was writing); or it might be that it is just the Central Bank which is acting as a monopolist. One can see that on the plane of generality on which Keynes was writing, it would be desirable to take such phenomena together. This, I believe, is what Keynes in substance did.

In order to do so ourselves, we shall need some terminology. Let us think of the financial system (not just the banking system) as consisting of two parts. There is a 'core' that is monopolistic, but the rest (which, on the geophysical analogy, I shall call the 'mantle') is competitive. So the core may be a Central Bank, while the rest of the banking system is in the mantle. Or we can allow the core to be more extensive, with nothing but the capital market, in some sense or other, left in the mantle. Or we can draw the line in some intermediate place, as in particular application may be convenient.

As Keynes himself puts the theory, it looks as if his core is large. For nothing appears to be left in the mantle except the capital market, and that is reduced to a market in long-term bonds. So all that is visible is the supply of money (core liabilities) and a single rate of interest that is determined in the mantle. Liquidity preference is the bridge between them.

Put in those terms, the Keynes model looks very special, and surely it is very special; but its essential features can be preserved if it is taken a little more generally. We shall need a name for the rest of the economy, outside both core and mantle; though it will include households and (presumably) government, I shall call it 'industry'.[24] It is assumed that *the core does not lend directly to industry* (being, admittedly, in this respect more like a Central Bank than a whole banking system). Then the core's liabilities are money, and its assets are *financial* securities, which are liabilities of the mantle. The mantle itself is of course composed of many entities, or firms; they will have debts to one another; but the *net* liabilities of the mantle as a whole must be composed of these financial securities, due to the core, together with any other financial securities, due to industry. Its net assets are *industrial* securities, *and money*. As for industry, its net liabilities (in a closed system) are these industrial securities (due to the mantle). Its net assets consist of real capital *plus* any financial securities (debts of the mantle) plus it holdings of money. In tabular form

	Liabilities	Assets
Core	Money $(M + m)$	Financial securities (F)
Mantle	Financial securities $(F + f)$	Industrial securities (I) + Money (m)
Industry	Industrial securities (I)	Real Assets (R) + Financial securities (f) + Money (M)

It will be noticed that if all three sectors are consolidated together, nothing remains except the real assets of industry (against which accountants would enter a notional liability, but since it is a pure residual, which can only change as an arithmetical consequence of other changes, it is here excluded).

The most obvious way in which this scheme differs from Keynes's is the distinction between financial and industrial securities, which I have drawn, but he does not draw. I do not myself see how it is to be avoided. For if the mantle holds money (m) which is non-interest-bearing, it is impossible that

[24] Thinking of the 'Industrial Circulation' in the *Treatise on Money*.

the rate of interest on industrial securities can be the same as on financial securities; if it was the same, it would follow that the mantle (which is assumed to be competitive) could not make a profit. The holding of money by the mantle, as Keynes very rightly saw, is essential, so long as one holds to the principle that the core lends only to the mantle. For otherwise the core would be unable to change the supply of money, on its own volition, so the supply of money could not be kept exogenous, as Keynes wishes to keep it. So one must distinguish between financial and industrial securities, because they must (normally) yield different rates of interest. Keynes neglected the difference, in this following Wicksell. But it does not appear that he had any right to follow Wicksell, in assuming a single rate of interest, while he was making the supply of money exogenous.

The matter is of much more than formal importance. Keynes's *single* rate of interest is a long-term rate. (His 'speculative' demand for money arises as a consequence of there being no way of lending, in his model, except lending long; so the 'bear' of long-term securities has to hold money idle, and cannot lend it short, as he would surely be likely to do, at least to a considerable extent, in practice.) The reason why Keynes laid such stress on long lending is clear. He was convinced that the principal determinant of spending, in 'industry', is the rate of *fixed capital investment*, investment in durable goods; and that, he thought, must be financed by long borrowing. But why must it be so financed? Or to what extent must it be so financed?

In our generalized model, the answer is obvious. If industry increases its holding of real assets (R), either its holding of money (M) must be diminished, or its holding of financial securities (f) must be diminished, or its borrowing (I) must be increased. If the investment is financed in either of the former ways, the investor's liquidity (his ability to react, by himself, independently of the consent of others, to unforeseen demands upon him) is diminished, and it is diminished to the full extent of the additional expenditure; while if he borrows (I)

there is no direct effect on his liquidity—only an indirect effect, through a possible repercussion on his ability to raise further loans. It seems safe to assume that this will be smaller than the other. It follows that ability to borrow will facilitate investment, since it makes it possible for investment to be undertaken with less loss of liquidity. But that is by no means all.

It must be emphasized that all of the items in our table are in value terms. Thus R may increase, either by real investment—a real addition to the stock of net assets—or by a mere rise in prices, as in a property boom. Keynes, it is clear, was chiefly thinking of the former case, and we will begin by following him.

Real investment does not begin as an addition to the stock of real assets; it begins as expenditure, of which the addition to the stock of real assets is a consequence. The expenditure is expenditure of money. It cannot come, to any great extent, from the already existing M, industry's already existing money holding; for nearly all of that must be supposed to be already occupied in circulating existing output, which (it is supposed) by the investment is to be *increased*. Though there will be leaks (such as are studied in the Multiplier theory), the net effect of increased real investment must be the absorption of money into industry (the other side to what Hume observed so long ago). So M is not really available for the financing of the investment, as might have appeared at first sight. M, in fact, will have to be increased.

There remain two alternatives—increasing I and diminishing f. Each of these will directly affect the liquidity of the mantle, since it is only from the mantle that the additional money can be drawn. In the former case, from the point of view of the mantle I is increased and m diminished; the effect is confined to the assets side, but on the assets side there is a sharp fall in liquidity. In the latter case, m is diminished and f is diminished; though the fall in m diminishes the liquidity of the mantle, by the fall in f its liquidity is increased. It follows that the liquidity of the mantle will be less reduced in the latter than in the former case. But in each case it will be reduced.

I now return for a moment to the property boom, where the position appears to be substantially different. One can see how this is if one reflects that it is possible for there to be a large rise in property values with hardly any *transactions*. Potential buyers put up their bids, and potential sellers put up their retention prices; there was no dealing at the lower prices and no dealing at the higher, yet prices rise. In practice, of course, there will always be some dealing, and more money gets locked up, on the way between buyer and seller, when prices are high than when they are low. But the amount of this money depends on the volume of transactions, not on the total value of the assets in question, so it may not be considerable. Besides, it is money which can be advanced by the mantle at small sacrifice in liquidity, since each single advance will soon be repaid. As a first approximation, it may thus be left out of account.[25]

We may therefore sum up. An increase in real investment, with constant supply of money $(M + m)$, must reduce liquidity somewhere. If the investment is financed by borrowing, the main loss in liquidity falls on the mantle; if by drawing on reserves, .the main loss falls on industry itself. If either has ample reserves, the loss in liquidity can be borne; it will in fact be distributed among sectors so that the sector which is better able to bear it will bear relatively more. This is a major way in which interest rates come into the story, for, in the choice between methods of financing, the interest charged (or given up) will always be an important consideration. But for the rest one need pay little attention to interest rates, changes in which emerge as consequences of changes in liquidity.

It will be noticed that the Keynes monetary model, as thus reinterpreted, does not seem to differ so very much (at least formally) from the Classical model as it was developed in the first section of this paper. It does appear to be more like the Classical model than it is like the Wicksell model. It is indeed

[25] I do not forget the money that was supposed to be 'locked up' in the Wall Street boom of 1929.

hard to see that there is anything in Keynes which corresponds to the 'equilibrium path'; but, as we have seen, Keynes was not interested in that kind of equilibrium. Nevertheless, so long as the supply of money is determined exogenously,[26] there still is a *ceiling*, of classical type. As in the classical case, the system does not have to be on its ceiling; positions (which Keynes would call equilibria) that are below the ceiling are possible and indeed likely. Even in the classical model (as we saw) the existence of a *floor* is hard to demonstrate; on this matter, notoriously, Keynes had greater doubts than his predecessors. It may be that this was a consequence of the greater sophistication of the financial system with which he was dealing. Because it was more sophisticated, it was also more brittle; so some of its principles were likely to snap if exposed to a strain.

We have nevertheless done injustice to Keynes in making him so classical, or even so semi-classical. For we have left out employment! The most than can be determined by a monetary theory, such as we have been discussing, is effective demand (*PQ*, or *Y* as Keynes calls it). One can envisage the possibility of a relation between the money value of output and that part of it which consists of wages, the 'wage bill'. But the wage-bill does not determine employment until we know the wage, or rather the average wage, of labour. That has to be brought in.

Keynes brought it in by working in wage-units, measuring effective demand in wage-units (*PQ/w* instead of *PQ*). This was no more than an expository device, and it has not been found by later expositors to be a useful device. It obliges one to turn intellectual somersaults and, what is worse, it confuses the issue. For it conceals the fact that Keynes is making an assumption; he is assuming that the wage-rate, or wage-system, is exogenous: another exogenous variable. If the sole effect of an increase in effective demand (in money terms), raising the wage-bill (in money terms), was to raise the money wage,

[26] Not that it need be kept constant, but that it moves in a way that is determined externally.

instead of raising employment, the Keynesian system would collapse. The model would always be at (Keynesian) full employment, whether there was little unemployment or much unemployment, in the practical sense.

The behaviour of wages is therefore critical. Now in the Great Depression, which Keynes had just behind him, there had indeed been some fall in money wages, but it was insignificant compared with the rise in unemployment. (That was so almost everywhere, in industrial countries.) It seemed therefore reasonable, and at the time it surely was very reasonable, to treat the effect on employment as the main effect. Though an effect on wages could be kept in as a qualification (and the wage-unit device does enable Keynes to keep it in as a qualification), the centre of the Keynes system is surely a model in which, at levels of employment less than full employment, the money wage does not change.

That keeps employment depending on PQ (in money terms). We may think of the economy, at a given time, as being confronted with a range, or series, of possible Keynesian equilibria, which can be arranged according to the value of PQ. At less than full employment, a change in PQ will mainly change Q, changing P relatively little. But when full employment is reached, Q can increase no further, so the main effect of a further increase in PQ must be on P. This relation between P and Q could evidently be drawn out as a curve—the 'supply curve of output', a concept which we do in fact find in Keynes.[27]

In the simplest case, that in which the wage-rate remains constant as long as there is unemployment (and in which the productivity of labour is the same, whatever the level of employment, while prices are formed from labour costs by a constant mark-up, which is unaffected by the level of employment), the supply curve will consist of two distinct parts (Fig. 2a). At less than full employment it will be horizontal (P_0F); at full employment it will be vertical (FF'). There are

[27] *General Theory*, pp. 292ff.

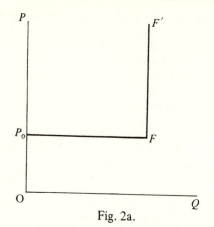

Fig. 2a.

just these two states of the economy; it must be in one or the other.[28]

Though this simple form of the Keynesian supply curve has played its part in history ('Full Employment without inflation' must presumably be interpreted as in injunction to find ways of reaching the point F and staying there), Keynes himself was not so simple-minded. He expressly allowed for the possibility that the wage would rise as full employment was approached, and for the possibility that there might be shortages of other inputs, so that the mark-up would increase; these would cause the curve to be rounded off, as in Fig. 2b. It will be noticed that in Fig. 2b there are no longer just two states of the economy; there is an intermediate state, which may be important. On the 'bend' one can still have more employment by expanding PQ, but only at the expense of more inflation; there is a 'trade-off' between them,

[28] It is perhaps worth noticing that we do not have to assume that wages shoot up along FF'. If the constant mark-up is maintained, that will indeed happen; but the rise in prices on FF' does not depend on that. As soon as Q has reached its maximum, a further rise in PQ must raise prices; it must do so, however the increased money value is distributed, between labour incomes and others.

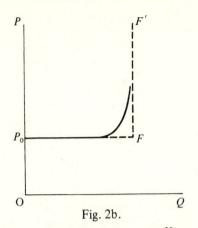

Fig. 2b.

as in later years we have so often been told. [29]

If the curve is asymptotic to FF', as I have drawn it (and this seems the natural way to take it) it follows that Full Employment is, strictly, out of reach. It remains the benchmark, but it is unattainable. This is a paradox which not only illuminates much of the subsequent course of Keynesian economies, but serves also to identify an essential feature of the *General Theory* itself.

'The *General Theory of Employment* is the Economics of

[29] One could further amend the supply curve by admitting the possibility that productivity might be less, or the mark-up larger, when un unemployment was large than when it was only moderate. This would cause the curve to slope downwards over some part of what would have been its horizontal segment, but it would not prevent a subsequent upward turn. Keynes did not make this amendment, but it is not inconsistent with his general approach.

Remember, however, that the points on the supply curve are alternative equilibria, to be reached, presumably, in much the same time. Thus if it is observed that in a practical case, between one date and another, there is a rise in employment and yet there is a fall in prices, one cannot conclude from that that a downward-sloping part of the curve is revealed. There may have been a fall in costs, or a fall in mark-up, arising from other causes than those of which the working is represented in the curve.

Depression.'[30] The possible equilibria, of a Keynesian system, are limited by a Full Employment constraint; but the system is always within that constraint, so it is always, in that sense, 'depressed'. It is similarly limited by a monetary constraint; but it is also, always, within that constraint—so it is 'depressed' in that sense too. Keynes is not just showing that 'Unemployment equilibrium' is possible; he is also showing that it is inevitable. It is inevitable, in his system (with the assumptions that he is making), that there should be idle labour, and it is also inevitable that there should be idle money.

Actual equilibrium must be under both ceilings; but it makes a great deal of difference what the relative position of the ceilings is. If the monetary ceiling is the lower, approach to Full Employment is prevented by scarcity of money; but by an increase in the money supply that constraint can be removed. Yet the mere removal (or raising) of the monetary ceiling does not automatically increase employment; for additional money can readily be absorbed in idle balances, and (if nothing else happens) it probably will be. That is Keynes's diagnosis of the conditions he thought to be 'normal'; it is not inconsistent with the view that a raising of the monetary ceiling, in conditions which approach Full Employment, will feed inflation.

We must remember the circumstances in which Keynes was writing. As I have insisted, it is to the international economy that a closed-system theory must refer, so it is to the international economy that we must look. It is not easy, in the international economy of the 1930s, to identify a monetary 'core', but the Central Banks of the main countries were still looking to their gold reserves, so that a bank money, based on gold, will still do as a 'core' money. It had certainly been true in the late 1920s, and up to the fall in the pound in December

---

[30] 'Mr. Keynes and the Classics' (*Econometrica*, 1937), last sentence. When reprinting that paper in *Critical Essays*, I suppressed this last sentence, for I did not want to stand by it in its obvious meaning. In the light of the present discussion, it can be given a better meaning, by which I am prepared to stand.

1931, that the trading world was (essentially) on a Gold Standard, with the total gold reserves of the main central banks as the fundamental monetary base. For some time after that, exchange fluctuations were large, but by 1935 the old relations between currencies seemed on the way to being re-established. Their relation to gold was nevertheless substantially different. Between April 1933 and January 1934 (when a fixed value of the dollar, in terms of gold, was re-established) the dollar was reduced to about three-fifths of its previous gold value; when the dollar–sterling exchange appeared to settle at near its old parity, the pound could be reckoned to be devalued, in terms of gold, in the same proportion. The new position could thus be described (approximately) as one in which the size of the monetary base had been written up by two-thirds. So the value of output, in the 'closed' international system, that could be financed without strain, seemed to be substantially increased.

The monetary brake had been taken off, but recovery, none the less, was tardy. These were the conditions in which Keynes was writing, so one can understand how it was that there was a turning-over, from monetary measures to more direct forms of stimulus, a turning-over which I think one can detect to have occurred in the course of writing the book. That was certainly how it came to be read. It should, however, be noticed that it would still have been possible, within the bounds of the theory, for the situation of that time to be read in another way. Keynes himself had shown why it was that the *long* rate of interest, on which he had relied, must respond to monetary ease rather slowly; that is in fact what happened, in Britain and in America, between 1932-3 and 1935. But why should there not be the same kind of lag on the other side? If one had recognized, as Keynes (on his own principles) surely ought to have recognized, that there are liquidity elements which affect decisions in 'industry', not just in the financial markets (our 'mantle'), it could have been seen that there were similar reasons why real investment should react to monetary *and financial* ease rather slowly. There had been a great shock. Industrialists, as well as financiers, had to recover; their wounds had to heal; they had to be able to see their way forward; all that had to be done before the economic system could begin to function in a 'normal' manner.

But that is more like Wicksell's point of view (or Robertson's) than Keynes's. Keynes, and his followers, were in more of a hurry.

(iv) Ourselves

I come at last to the topical question that was set at the beginning of this paper. How much is to be learned from the monetary theories we have been examining, considered in the way we have been examining them, that can have any relevance today? They were put forward, it has been shown, in very different conditions from ours; may they nevertheless, even if only by contrast, have something for us now?

These theories, I have emphasized, were theories of a closed system; so it must be the world economy (or what we may call the trading-world economy) to which they have to refer. It is less easy for us than it was in the days of Gold Standards, to think in terms of a world-wide monetary system; but some at least of the problems which concern us are world problems, so a closed-economy theory need not on that account be wholly out of date. Moderately, but continually, rising prices, with a high level of unemployment, were characteristic—on a world scale—of what has been called the Bretton Woods period, that lasted from some time in the 1950s to the dollar crisis of 1971; a much more rapid inflation of prices, with much worse employment, has been characteristic—again on a world scale—of what has happened since. Why did prices behave as they did during the Bretton Woods period? and why has there been the subsequent acceleration? Why have there been these changes in employment behaviour? These are large questions; but they are questions with which our present approach may be fitted to deal.

We began with the *Classical Quantity theory*; and it will be appropriate to begin with it again. For it has become very fashionable to go back to Quantity of Money; if only that could be controlled, (say our Monetarists) inflation would be cured. It was for the sake of throwing light upon that contention that I began this study with a very simple 'hard money' case, in which there was no doubt that the supply of money was controlled, controlled (as far as the institutions of that economy were concerned) by natural forces, which no one could do anything about. Monetarism, in such an economy, would not be a policy; it would be a fact. Even then (as I showed), although the value of that output could not rise beyond a limit, it could fall below that limit. Fluctuations were possible (about an equilibrium path, which was below the *ceiling*); and it was quite likely that when the value of output encountered its ceiling, there would be a crisis, which would not be nice. (See p. 57, above). Such crises were made more likely by the rise of banking, but they could arise, even in the absence of banking. Yet though banking, if uncontrolled, made crises more violent, the concentration of credit (which was implied in the growth of a banking *system*) did hold out a hope that by suitable policy, exercised within the system, the fluctuations might be mitigated. The economy might be held closer to its equilibrium path.

That, however, assumed that the ceiling was there, and could not be moved. It assumed that it was known that the ceiling could not be moved. It was because of that knowledge that measures of stabilization had a chance to work.[31] Booms were felt to be booms, and slumps were felt to be slumps; prices were high in the one and low in the other, relatively to a *normal* level. As long as that persisted, there was a 'tendency to equilibrium', a tendency which wise credit policy could, in principle, help.

We have seen how it was that in the monetary turmoil of

[31] For discussion of a related point, see pp. 128–9 below.

the thirties, the metallic base was weakened; already, at that time, some of its authority was lost. In the Bretton Woods period, that went much further. It was generally recognized, during that period, that the world was *de facto* on a dollar standard. Though the dollar was formally convertible into gold, it was the dollar not gold that was the primary money. So the supply of money, throughout the trading world, was no longer limited by natural forces, as in Classical days. If (to use our language) the value of output were to rise so as to encounter the Ceiling, it was taken for granted that the Ceiling would be moved. That was a big step towards the pure credit economy, such as Wicksell had analysed. It is not surprising that the actual economy began to work in something like a Wicksellian way.

It is not hard to work out what Wicksell would have said about it. In his day, prices were falling; he concluded, in accordance with this theory, that the market rate of interest was not being reduced as fast as the natural rate was falling. During the Bretton Woods period, for a comparable length of time, prices were rising; the Wicksell theory would therefore be read as indicating that market rates of interest were not being raised fast enough. It is indeed very possible that there was a first phase when a lagged response of interest rates did feed the inflation; but to ascribe the whole experience of the fifties and sixties to that cause would surely over-estimate the importance of banking policy. There must have been other forces at work; into the revised version of Wicksell which we have based on Myrdal they can, however, find a place.

In that version, it will be remembered, there was no single price-index, constancy of which would ensure 'equilibrium'; there was not even any particular course of money prices which could necessarily be dignified with the title of an equilibrium course. Various equilibrium courses of prices were possible; in order to give one of them precedence over another one had to fall back on non-monetary considerations. The only ground on which one of these paths could be judged to be superior to another was that, in the institutional state of the economy, it was easier to carry it through.

What that preferred path should be could hardly be described by bankers; it would surely be decided for them. All they would be able to do, by 'keeping the market rate of interest in line with the natural rate'—now the natural rate of that particular path—would be to see that finance was not an *additional* source of disturbance. This would clearly mean that, in conditions of inflation, market rates of interest must rise, correspondingly; if they do not do so, they feed the inflation, unnecessarily. On this view of the matter that is about as much as, from monetary policy alone, one can expect.

We get this (rather negative) result from Myrdal; we can give more substance to it if we combine it with what can be learned from Keynes.

Let us go back to Keynes's 'supply curve of output' (Fig. 2 above). But now, since we are here concerned with a Wicksell-type long-period problem, not with Keynes's short-period problem, let us take up that supply curve rather differently. Instead of relating level of prices (P) to level of output (Q), our new curve shall relate their *rates of changes over time* (p and q). Thus what is measured on the vertical axis of Fig. 3 (in each of its forms) is the rate of change of some price-index, the *rate of inflation*. What is measured on the horizontal axis is the rate of change of real output, what is commonly called *the growth rate*. These axes (Op and Oq) have now a special significance. Points on Oq ($p = O$) are points of zero inflation; points on Op ($q = O$) are points of zero growth.

As in Keynes, a more expansionary policy (whether monetary or budgetary—the resultant of the effects of the various countries' budgets) is shown by a movement to the right along the curve.[32] It must, however, be insisted that the points on the new curve are alternative equilibria (relatively long-term equilibria, of Wicksell–Myrdal type, not short-term equilibria

---

[32] More strictly, a movement which is such as to increase $p + q$; for growth rate of PQ = growth rate of P + growth rate of Q.

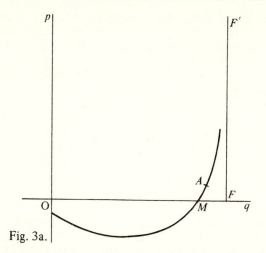

Fig. 3a.

like Keynes's). Thus nothing is shown on the diagram about the passage from one of these equilibria to another. What are shown are alternative possibilities.

What can be said about the shape of this curve—the 'growth supply curve' we may perhaps call it? It is not the same as the Keynes curve, so it needs to be checked over separately.

It is clear, in the first place, that there must be a barrier, corresponding to Keynes's Full Employment. There must, that is to say, be a maximum physical growth rate which is attainable by expansion; we can draw it as FF' on our new diagram, as we did in that which we took from him. Any attempt to increase the rate of growth beyond that point must result in indefinite inflation.[33]

---

[33] I do not mean to exclude the possibility that the rate of growth might be increased above OF by measures of reorganization which are not simply expansionary measures. These, however, are not our present concern.

Nor would I exclude the possibility, indeed probability, that expansionary measures might be taken so far as to diminish efficiency. This

What happens at lower growth rates depends on the behaviour of markets, of the labour market and of product markets. Let us begin by making the Keynesian assumption (or perhaps one should say the 'vulgar-Keynesian' assumption) that the level of wages will be stationary at low levels of growth, but will rise as full employment is approached. Let us also suppose that prices are cost-determined, being fixed (at those low levels) at a constant mark-up over labour costs. These assumptions (which were made for the Keynes curve) will not necessarily give us the same shape of curve as we found for the Keynes curve, since here we must take account of changes in productivity. It is a fair assumption[34] that there is some relation between productivity and growth. With zero growth in output there might be some growth in productivity; but a higher growth in output (which must require higher investment to support it) may surely be taken to carry with it, at least up to a point, a higher rise in productivity. It follows that if prices are cost-determined, prices will be *lower* (again up to a point) the faster the rate of growth. That seems to give the shape of the curve that is drawn in Fig. 3a.

In these conditions, it will be seen, there is an interesting point, marked M, where there is considerable growth, and yet there is no inflation. There would be some unemployment at M, but it is possible that it might not be very serious. (It might then be said that at M there is a 'natural rate of unemployment.) Why should it not have been possible just to go to M and stay there?

One reason is evident. Once it is understood that more expansionary policies can reduce unemployment, a zero-inflation policy is not tenable politically. So long as inflation is moderate, it is regarded as a lesser evil than even moderate

---

could be shown on the diagram by making the curve turn backwards as it approached FF', instead of reaching, or becoming asymptotic to, it. It is however sufficient for my argument to stop the curve short of that.

[34] As Kaldor has often reminded us.

unemployment. So 'political equilibrium' must be found at a point to the right of M (A in Fig. 3a). And that is where, in the Bretton Woods period, it seems to have been found.

But we can dig deeper than that. It is impossible to believe that the growth in productivity could be uniform. There must be some sectors where productivity is increasing relatively rapidly, while there are others in which measurable growth in productivity can hardly occur. Thus the way in which one is tempted to read the diagram—reckoning that at M there are rising money incomes, so that all that has to be determined is the division of the gain between wages and profits—will not do.

Keep our assumption that the profit mark-up is constant. And suppose that the rise in wages is uniform between industries. (There will be additional troubles if these assumptions do not hold.) Even so, it will be necessary for prices in the *fast* industries to fall, relatively to those in the slow; so a constant general price-level can only be achieved if the *slow* prices rise, and the *fast* prices fall, so as to give no change on the average. That cannot be easy to arrange; to keep up just sufficient pressure to keep the *fast* prices falling fast enough.

We shall find the issue easier to recognize if we allow ourselves to look at it in national terms. Consider a model consisting of two countries, with different rates of increase of productivity; we will label them according to this difference, calling them *Fast* and *Slow* respectively. In each country there are two sectors, one of them an 'international' sector, producing goods that are tradeable between the countries; the other a 'domestic' sector, producing non-tradeables. We will suppose (not so very unrealistically) that in the domestic sector of each country productivity is not changing; the growth in productivity (the differential growth in productivity) occurs in the international sector only.

If, within each country, resources are freely transferable between sectors, 'international' prices must be falling relatively to 'domestic', the rate of (relative) price-fall depending on the rate of productivity increase in the 'international' sector. If the two countries are on a common standard, and there are no significant obstacles to trade between them, the prices of 'international' goods must be more or less the same in each country; let p_i be the *rate* at which this 'international' price-level is increasing (p_i may of course be negative). Then if h_F is the rate of productivity increase in 'international' production in Fast, the rate at which 'domestic' prices must be rising in Fast is $p_i + h_F$; and the over-all rate of price-rise in Fast will be some average between this and p_i, which may be written $p_i + k_F h_F$. The over-all rate of price-rise in Slow will be similarly $p_i + k_S h_S$. Thus if the k's (which depend upon the share of internationally traded goods in the total production of the country in question) are much the same in the two countries, the over-all level of prices in Fast will need to be rising, relatively to that in Slow, by $k (h_F - h_S)$.

This calculation is based upon far too many simplifying assumptions to be more than suggestive; but it is evident that the simplifications can be relaxed a good deal and, at least in strong cases, the main conclusion will remain. If there is a great difference between the rates of growth in productivity in Fast and Slow, in the products in which they are competitive, prices in Fast must rise, relatively to those in Slow, if any balance is to be kept in the trade between them. So Slow can only succeed in maintaining stable prices, in a common money, if prices in Fast rise quite rapidly; while if that 'inflation' is resisted in Fast, Slow must get into trouble. In international terms, this has become familiar; it has been widely used as an argument against fixed exchanges. It should, however, be observed that just the same disequilibrium can arise within a single country, when *fast* and *slow* sectors are in competition with one another. And it should also be observed that the phenomenon is essentially a phenomenon of rapid growth—which almost inevitably carries great disparities in growth rates with it.

During the Bretton Woods period the rates of growth that were achieved by the Fasts of this world were large, in historical terms quite unusually large; it is therefore not surprising that something like the preceding analysis seems to apply.

It was only if there was a fair degree of 'inflation' in the system as a whole that the situation of the Slows could be tolerable; but the more successful the Fasts were in controlling their inflation, the more difficult the position of the Slows became. That is pretty well what happened in the Bretton Woods period;[35] but we can get an even better fit if we make a further amendment.

We have been (tacitly) assuming, in our Fast and Slow story, that the balance of payments between them is kept in balance. In the end it will have to balance; but one can understand that there is likely to be an interim during which the situation is alleviated by Slow running an adverse balance—Fast in effect lending to Slow. It is quite likely to be the case that while the imbalance lasts, it will increase the rate of price-rise in *both* countries. This is primarily because Fast, finding its abundant production easier to sell, is under diminished pressure to reduce the prices of its 'international' goods; thus the (common) price-level of international goods can rise more rapidly, or fall less. This is likely to offset any 'deflationary' effect of its foreign lending on Fast; while in Slow there will be an inflationary, or anti-deflationary, effect, quite apart from what happens to the international goods price-level.[36]

---

[35] Japan, with its exceptionally high growth rate, was a leading example of a Fast country. Prices rose in Japan quite exceptionally during the sixties, though the yen remained exceptionally strong.

[36] It may be useful to set this out in formal terms. I take the case of Slow, presumed to have an adverse balance; the analysis can be extended to cover Fast just by change of sign.

Write the country's output of international goods Q_i, of domestic goods Q_d. Let cost per unit of the former be C_i, of the latter C_d. Then total earnings of the country's factors of production are

$$C_i Q_i + C_d Q_d.$$

Let the prices per unit of the two sorts of goods be P_i and P_d (as will be seen, we have to distinguish). Then the market value of the total production is

$$P_i Q_i + P_d Q_d.$$

Write B for the *volume* of net imports (financed by the balance-of-payments deficit); we may take it that these are internationally traded

We need hardly more than this to make the general position, in the Bretton Woods period, quite readily intelligible. For we have now another reason why the equilibrium of the system should be such as was shown by the point A in Fig. 3a—inflation, but moderate inflation. We can also see why this condition was consistent with a quite high level of employment. There could be high employment because of the rapid rise in productivity; for that made it possible to have high employment with so modest a rise in prices.

Nothing particular need be said, in order to get this result, on whether the inflation was demand-determined, or cost-determined—the familiar distinction. Either of them works in much the same way. It is implied in our argument that at M, and still more at A, there are rising money incomes—rising incomes not only in the sectors where the rise in productivity is occurring, but in the others too. Nothing need be said about the mechanism by which the rise in money incomes is transmitted from the former to the latter. It could be on the demand side—rising income from the production of tradeables increasing demand for non-tradeables; or it could be on the supply side, prices having to rise in the latter in order that re-

goods, with price P_i. Then total expenditure (we need not distinguish between consumption and investment expenditure) is
$$P_i (Q_i + B) + P_d Q_d$$
and this must be equal to total earnings.

Assume that $P_d = C_d$. Then
$$P_i (Q_i + B) = C_i Q_i,$$
so $C_i > P_i$; there are losses in the deficit country's production of international goods (which may be financed by subsidies or in other ways—it does not matter how they are financed). A positive B enables the deficit country to maintain C_i above P_i; if C_d moves with C_i (by transferability of factors between sectors or in other ways) the over-all price-level, which is an average of P_i and Pd ($= C_d$) will be *raised* in relation to P_i.

The same argument shows that the over-all price-level in the surplus country will be *lowered*, relatively to P_i. Thus, with fixed exchange-rates, disequilibrium in the balance of payments reduces the price-disparity; while (as stated above) it also tends to raise P_i, thus diminishing the pressure on the deficit country in that way also.

sources should not be drawn (too much) away from them to the former. Or it could be that rising prices, when they have continued sufficiently, engender an expectation of further rises; that this influences wage-bargaining; so there is an 'independent wage-push' from that cause (or perhaps from other causes). I find it hard to believe that the *general* price-rise, in the Bretton Woods period, was sufficient to cause this last to be of major importance—on a world scale; though doubtless there were particular countries in which this was not so.[37] But we had better keep it in mind, as we shall want it later.

If 'independent wage-push' is important, it will change our curve. So far we have kept the assumption that at low rates of growth, the level of wages is constant; but that (as Keynes well knew) can be no more than an empirical assumption—it does not have to hold. If there were an independent wage-push, it would shift the whole of our growth-supply curve upwards (Fig. 3b). The 'optimum' position M would then

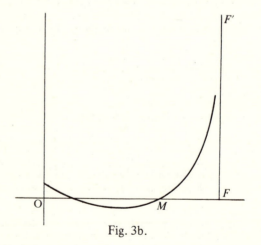

Fig. 3b.

---

[37] Britain? Australia?

move to the left, so that the 'natural rate of unemployment' would increase; and indeed, with a wage-push that was sufficiently strong, there would be no level of unemployment which would prevent inflation.

For the world economy, in the Bretton Woods period, this was surely no more than a theoretical possibility. It becomes, I believe, much more than that—later on.

So let us pass on. The strains to which the Bretton Woods system was exposed have been indicated; and it also has been shown how, over time, they were likely to build up. The devaluation of sterling, in 1967, was perhaps the first crack; but sterling was no longer so important as it had been earlier, so if that had stood by itself, it could probably have been absorbed. The dollar crisis was a different matter.

It had then become clear that the United States, also, was a Slow; or at least not Fast enough for the responsibilities that it had undertaken. So it also passed through a phase of adverse balance. For a while (as, in terms of the analysis just set out, we should expect) this helped. But it was carried so far that reputation was damaged. The dollar had been the key currency, the safest currency, the pivot on which the credit economy turned. And now it was uncertain whether the dollar was quite so safe. Though there was no obvious rival, the doubt persisted. So the time came when the pivot shifted, and the fixed exchange rates (based on the dollar) departed.

It might have been expected (and by many economists it clearly was expected) that 'floating', by making it harder for the Fast countries to sell their exports, would in those countries have a deflationary effect; and though the effect on prices in the Slow countries (when prices were measured in terms of their now depreciated currencies) might well be different, there would still be a general fall in prices, when measured in terms of the Fast countries' currencies, relatively undepreciated. On this view, therefore, (inflation being measured in terms of non-depreciated currencies) there should have been a movement, on our diagram, from A back towards M—a check to inflation, at the expense of a fall in employment. But things did not work out like that. Why?

A devaluation, by a non-key country (such as the British in 1967) must have indeed have this effect, to an extent proportional to that country's importance; for that country would itself be obliged to restrain demand, in order to make sure that its devalued exchange rate would stick. The floating of the dollar was different. There was no new rate which had to be defended. The old fixed-rate system was in ruins, so it had to be put about, in order to make the new system acceptable, that floating was itself a good thing—that a constraint, which had formerly been an unwarrantable hindrance to expansion, was now removed. There was thus no post-devaluation cut-back in America, and others were not slow to follow the American example.

The result was a very general boom. But it was a very short-lived boom, lasting hardly more than a year. There is no doubt what killed it. The early seventies were the end of an epoch, not only in the way that we have been discussing, but also in another.

This is no place to recount the history—the harvest failures of 1972, the Oil Squeeze of 1973, and the shortages of industrial raw materials which appeared at about the same time. What we have here to do is to find a place for these things, and for their consequences, in the theory.

The first of the things which is called in question by this most recent experience is the Keynesian identification of the limit to growth with Full Employment of Labour. What has now to be faced is the possibility that the limit might be set by something else. If there are two possible barriers, the one which is first reached is the one which will be effective. It could thus be that in the Bretton Woods period, the Full Employment barrier was indeed the effective barrier; but that since then the effective barrier has been different. Full Employment, at the high growth rates of the Bretton Woods period, cannot now be reached, since the supplies of primary products that would be needed to support it are not available.

It is indeed remarkable that those high rates of growth

could go on so long, without causing more of a strain on the primary product side; one might have expected more sign of Diminishing Returns. There were many, of course, who were predicting a strain—the populationists from whom we have heard so much. It could be that what has happened is that Malthus, long kept waiting in the wings, has at last arrived. But it could also be that the exceptional expansion of 1972–3 imposed an exceptional strain; in the long run supplies are still expansible, but they could not expand, for the moment, at the exceptional rate required. Either view is possible; it is not necessary, in this place, to try to pronounce between them, since (for the time being) the situation resulting from either would be much the same.

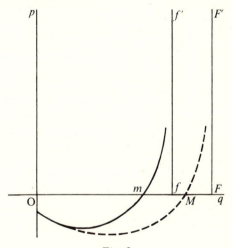

Fig. 3c.

Let us look at it on our diagram (now Fig. 3c). In this version I exclude any independent 'wage-push'. Thus, if there were no new constraint, the growth supply curve could still take the form it took in Fig. 3a, here reproduced as the dotted curve. When the new constraint becomes effective (at

ff') the curve shifts, as shown. There is still a 'trade-off' between inflation and unemployment, but now it is a much less favourable 'trade-off'. The former position (A) is now out of reach; any attempt to reach it will result in more severe inflation, without remedying the more severe unemployment.[38]

That shows part of what has happened, but we can go a good deal further. It is not just the limit to expansion, but also the working of markets, which must be looked at again.

We have, so far, on that been quite Keynesian, even conventionally Keynesian. We have allowed ourselves to think of prices as being determined by costs; accepting, nevertheless, as Keynes did, that costs would probably rise (because wages rose) and the mark-up would probably rise, as Full Employment was approached. That, in the new conditions, is clearly insufficient. We must, at the least, incorporate a primary product sector, which works in a different way.

There are doubtless many kinds of pricing behaviour. It is quite proper to classify them in different ways, for different purposes. So it is quite proper to have one theory of pricing, when one is dealing with 'micro' problems (the Theory of the Firm), and another for use in 'macro' problems, such as those we are considering here. The latter must surely be kept very simple, with no more distinctions than are necessary. It would be best if we could get by with just one distinction. It is fortunate that there is a well-tried distinction which looks as if it would serve.

It is just the traditional (classical or Marshallian) distinction between diminishing cost and increasing cost industries; the latter being identified with primary production, the former with the manufacturing production which Keynes must have had (largely) in mind. In increasing cost industries, where prices that are equal to marginal costs can still yield a sufficient surplus, we can get by with the conventional supply and

[38] Whether or not M is out of reach depends, of course, upon the severity of the primary product check.

demand apparatus; but in diminishing cost industries, that will not do. If a firm is to survive, it must sell at a price which exceeds its marginal costs; it must indeed sell at a price which exceeds its (higher) average costs; but how much the excess will be cannot easily be determined. It nevertheless seems proper to think of prices in these industries as being determined (substantially) by costs, in what we have called the conventional Keynesian manner.[39] So we have two sectors, a primary sector in which prices are determined by demand and supply,[40] and a secondary sector, in which prices are cost-determined.

In the primary sector, accordingly, there is an upward-sloping supply curve of output; but here also there are increases in productivity. Thus so long as the increase in demand does not outstrip the rise in productivity, there is no reason why prices should rise. In the short run, however, supply is inelastic; so if the rate at which demand expands exceeds the rate at which productivity expands, prices will rise sharply. And since the prices of primary products enter into the costs of manufactures, a rise in primary product prices communicates itself to manufacturing product prices, leading to a general rise. This, in effect, is already shown in Fig. 3c.

But that clearly is not all that has happened. Though the accelerated rise in prices took its origin in the primary product sector, the effect has been greater than could be attributed, directly, to the rise in the prices of primary products. And the accelerated inflation has persisted, even after 1974, when diminished activity diminished the strain on the primary product markets. There is surely something else—the reaction

---

[39] The distinction here drawn between 'industries' is parallel to that which I drew in my Helsinki lectures (*The Crisis in Keynesian Economics*, 1973) between fixprice and flexprice markets; but since the latter was a short-period distinction, relating to stock holding, while this is a long-period distinction, the two are not exactly the same.

[40] This need not, and of course must not, exclude the possibility of monopolistic action in a primary product market; as for instance the Oil Cartel.

on wages, of which we have not yet taken account. Money wages have also increased, at a far faster rate than in the sixties; and this, by raising the costs of manufacturing industry, has raised prices further. This has happened, it will be noticed, not only in countries with strong Trade Unions, but fairly generally.

I do not think that this is hard to understand. It is quite wrong to think of the labour market as being similar to a primary product market, in which price is set by demand and supply. Even the more sophisticated versions of wage theory, which attribute the rate of rise in wages to variations in the balance between unemployment and unfilled vacancies, are on the wrong track. The contract of employment, at least in so far as the more important parts of the labour market are concerned, is an arrangement under which people have to work together; they will not work together efficiently unless the terms of employment are felt to be fair, by both sides. The pursuit of fairness in labour relations has many difficult aspects (differentials for instance); but one of the clearest and least controversial of the demands which it makes is for continuity in standard of living. Thus, when there is a considerable rise in cost of living, it is felt, by both sides, that a rise in money wages is *fair*. That is the reason for indexation of wages, whether formal or informal. Whether or not it is formal, it must be expected to be present.[41]

[41] There is indeed a historical question about this, which deserves examination. It did evidently happen, in former times, say in the nineteenth century, that there were sharp increases in the cost of living, in particular years, due to harvest failures; but these do not appear, in those times, to have led to rises in money wages. The explanation may partly be that such rises in prices were known to be temporary, and their cause was very obvious; but perhaps it is more likely that there has been a long-term change in climate of opinion, in a more 'socialist' direction. If it was this last, the two wars would have been decisive catalysts. Wage-indexation, so far as Britain is concerned, seems to make its first appearance in World War I.

That socialist values should have come to have influence on the working of the labour market would not be at all surprising; but if they

Wage-indexation, however, though it steepens, indeed greatly steepens, the slope of the growth-supply curve, as drawn in Fig. 3c, does not change its general character. If activity were to be so greatly reduced as to prevent the rise in primary product prices, indexation should in principle make no difference; the same point m, which would be attainable without indexation, would also be attainable with it. But any increase in activity beyond m must then be accompanied by a rapid rise in prices in general, so that the growth-supply curve, though still passing through m, will rise even more rapidly to the right of m than it is shown in the figure as drawn. Any resistance to the fall in employment (which in itself is inevitable) will lead to more acute inflation.

Nor is that all. The states of the economy that are attainable, as a result of the movement of the barrier (to ff') are not only states of much less than full employment; they also have low growth rates. Thus the feasible rate of rise in real wages, also, is reduced. Long experience of rising real wages, in days of less restricted growth, may well have led to a continuance

---

are important there, may they not be of some importance in other markets also? One thinks not only of the public sector, and of the quasi-public sector, where the employer, being under political control, must have such things in mind; it is by no means impossible that they have come to have some importance in private industry also. This is a possibility which has been interestingly explored by Arthur Okun (*Inflation, its mechanics and welfare costs*, Brookings Papers, 1975). He uses a sectoral division very similar to that used here. His demand-and-supply markets he calls auction markets; his markets in which prices are cost-determined he calls 'customer' markets—because he holds that it is typical of such markets that prices are fixed in a way which at least purports to be *fair* between producer and customer. This leads, as he shows, to pricing by cost, since a rise in price due to a rise in cost can be 'explained' to the customer, while a rise in price that is due to an increase in demand cannot be explained in the same way. In an earlier version of the latter part of this essay, which is published in the Australian *Economic Record* (Dec. 1976) I gave a good deal of attention to this contention of Okun's. I do not wish to withdraw what I said in that place; but I have not stressed the point here, since I do not think it is essential to my argument.

of that rise becoming part of the 'requirement'; for that also can be represented as necessary for continuity. If this happens, it will have to be reckoned, unlike the indexation, as an 'independent wage-push'. I expressed the opinion that in pre-1970 conditions, independent wage-push was not likely to have been important, save perhaps in some particular countries and in particular circumstances. In conditions when the rate of growth is checked, one cannot be so sure.

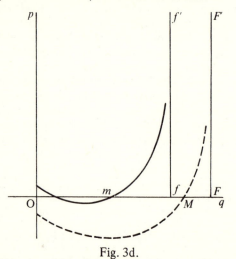

Fig. 3d.

Suppose it is important. The resulting situation will then be such as could be represented on our diagram by Fig. 3d. The whole of the growth-supply curve is displaced, in a 'north-westerly' direction. So long as that situation lasts, inflation is inevitable, and high unemployment is also inevitable. Neither can be cured by monetary policy, or by fiscal policy. All that can be done in these ways is to get less of one by having more of the other. But both, it may well be, are already intolerable!

One can get that far (if it is worth getting that far) without leaving the closed-economy model, which has been with us for so long. But of course that is still over-simplifying. One cannot really think of 'policy' selecting a 'point on a curve' as on my diagrams I have been making it appear to do. The trading world does not have a single government, with a single policy. And the I.M.F. is not a world Central Bank! There are many governments, with their own banks, acting independently. They affect each other; they are subject, in total, to the same constraints; but they are affected by the constraints in different ways.

It would clearly be possible, as a next step, to proceed (as before) to a two-country model. But since it is the relation between primary products and industrial products which is here at issue, one of the two countries should be a (net) exporter of a primary product, the other a (net) importer. The effect, in real terms, of a fall in the supply of the primary product, relatively to what it should have been on the old growth path, is familiar. There is bound to be a movement of the terms of trade in favour of the exporter; if demand is inelastic, at the old level of activity, the balance of payments will move, initially, in favour of the exporter and against the importer. This, in itself, makes for expansion of activity in the exporting country and contraction in the importing country; but as before we can go further.

As long as the imbalance remains, the exporter is in effect lending to the importer; and such lending, as we have seen,[42] makes for expansion of PQ in the system as a whole. Or what comes to the same thing, it is easier for the high price of the primary product to be maintained, while the importer is able to borrow in order to pay it. In the case of a temporary shortage, that may be very helpful; but if the shortage continues, it must become apparent that the imbalance cannot last. Even while the imbalance remains (statistically) the threat of its discontinuance depresses spirits, first in the importing country but in the end in the other also.

---

[42] Above, pp. 95–6.

One could go so far (and no doubt much further) with a two-country importer–exporter model; but that model, in its turn, would be over-simplifying. It needs, at the least, to be crossed with our other distinction; we need to distinguish between Fast and Slow, at least among importing countries. One would have to represent them as being in competition for the scarce supply of primary product, and one would expect that in that competition Fast would do better. The strain, which is ultimately due to what has happened in the primary product market, would thus be felt most severely by the Slow Importers.[43]

Our dismal diagram (Fig. 3d) was constructed to refer to a closed economy—the trading world as a whole; but it could also be applied, and perhaps more forcefully applied, to the case of a Slow Importer. Most forcefully indeed to the case of a Slow Importer which has reacted by turning in upon itself; making itself, as far as it can, into a closed economy; withdrawing, as far as it can, from the trading world. It surely does indicate that in the conditions supposed, that is not an easy way out.

But what way out is there? If there is no 'point on the curve' that is tolerable, the only thing is to move the 'curve'. What must be done is to work on the barriers. Neither of them need be taken for granted. Wage-inflation can be mitigated by labour-market policy; as time goes on, that should become less difficult, for it would have been the *change* from a more rapid to a slower rate of growth that was a main reason for the wage-inflation. As people become accustomed to the lower rate of rise in real wages, that has become inevitable, the pressure on that front may relax. But this, it may well be

[43] The United States, though not (as we have seen) particularly Fast, is not, on our classification, a net Importer. Thus America is not one of the countries that have experienced a particular stress. It has even been possible for the Americans to take advantage of the Depression, from which they have suffered like others, and so to go some way towards restoring the dollar as a key currency.

said, is no more than to accept defeat.

How much better it would be to work on the other barrier. Not simply to find ways of narrowing the gap between the constraints on output (FF' and ff' on our diagrams). The gap could be narrowed, and to some extent it is being narrowed, by working on FF', absorbing labour without expanding output—concealing unemployment. Such devices however are just another way, a worse way, of accepting defeat. What has to be done, in order to win through, is to ease the constraint on the primary product side. This could be eased, and it is quite likely that it will be eased, by straightforward productivity growth in the supply of primary products—increased efficiency in production from existing sources and the development of new sources of supply. If that happens, the Depression of the Seventies will have been no more than an episode. It could also be overcome by a weakening of the monopolistic tendencies which are apparent in so many of these markets—the Oil Cartel is no more than a leading example. Even if these fail, the constraint could be eased by changing production methods—changing the methods of production of existing commodities and changing the proportions in which commodities are produced—so as to use more labour and less primary product in production of equivalent value. Though this last may seem like a turning-back from the natural development of industrialism, which has so largely consisted in the massive substitution of natural resources (especially in the form of power) for the physical labour of human beings, it could be that the stage in industrial development which had that characteristic is quite properly ending.[44] If the pendulum should swing the other way, not back towards greater use of man as a beast of burden, but towards (relatively) greater use of his intelligence in the production of articles of superior quality, that would not be a defeat.

---

[44] Above pp. 25–39.

IV EXPECTED INFLATION*

We have been accustomed to classifying the causes of inflation into those which come from the side of demand and those which come from the side of cost—'demand-pull' and 'cost-push'. Demand inflation, we have learned, is likely to be accompanied, at least for a time, by over-full employment and at least apparently increasing production; cost-inflation, on the other hand, is not in itself a stimulus, so that it can well be accompanied with a low rate of growth. Neither the British nor the American situation, in 1969, looks like one of demand inflation; the British, at least, can fairly readily be analysed in cost inflation terms.

In practice, the cost inflation explanation usually reduces to ascribing the inflation to the aggressiveness of Trade Unions; but if this is followed through, we have to say that a rise in the rate of inflation is due to the Trade Unions having become more 'aggressive'. Why? There are certainly cases when there is an obvious reason. If real wages are falling, or if a rise which had become customary is failing to materialize, it is not surprising that there should be increased 'aggressiveness'. One can account in that way for much of what happens.

Yet it takes two to make a bargain—even a wage-bargain. It does not follow, because there is a reason why labour should extend its claims, that conditions will be such that the claim will be conceded. The willingness of employers to grant the rise in wages has also to be explained.

It is becoming fashionable, at this point, to lay great stress on the monetary aspect. How are employers to get the money

* An extract from an article, with the same title, which was published in the *Three Banks Review*, Sept. 1970. Reproduced by permission of the National and Commercial Banking Group Limited. I have not attempted to amend the remarks which are dated to that period, since they remain good illustrations of general principles. The substance of what I said still seems to be applicable.

to finance the increased money wages? If they knew they could not get the money, they would not yield so easily. There is an answer to cost inflation; it is monetary restraint.

At least in this simple form, I do not think the argument holds. For when employers grant rises in wages (the result of increased 'aggressiveness') they surely expect that they will soon be able to raise their selling prices to cover their increased costs. This still involves them in a financial problem, during the transition; but it is a limited problem. Even in conditions of some financial stringency, it can usually be dealt with, in some way or other. This is not to say that monetary restraint is ineffective; but it is unlikely to be effective in this particular way unless it is also effective in other ways—unless it is also restricting the (real) volume of business activity. No one questions that it is possible to stop inflation by administering a severe shock to credit; but the costs of that are such that it is only exceptionally that governments (and bankers) have been willing to face them.

There is, however, a more subtle form of the monetary (or monetarist) argument. The reason why businesses are so confident that they will be able to raise prices in the future is because they have become so accustomed to rising prices in the past. How solid this experience has become is at once apparent from the accompanying table. In all of these eight countries, over all of these six years, prices have been rising:

PERCENTAGE RISE IN CONSUMER PRICE-INDEX OVER TWO-YEAR PERIODS

	1963-65	1965-67	1967-69
U.K.	9	6	11
U.S.	4	6	11
France	7	6	12
Germany	7	4	5
Italy	10	7	5
Belgium	10	7	6
Sweden	12	8	6
Canada	5	8	9

sometimes (but rarely) at no more than 2 per cent per annum, most usually at about 3 per cent, and lately, in some most important cases, at 5 per cent. If one had carried the table further back, into the fifties, it would have been much the same story. Price-inflation, at some rate (still, it is true, for the most part a fairly modest rate) has become *normal*.

It is clear that rises in prices are now, quite generally, *expected*. I do not simply mean expected in the Gallup poll sense: that if people were asked whether they expected prices to rise, say over the next five years, they would reply in the affirmative. No doubt they would. It is much more important that large sections of the community have adjusted themselves, in their behaviour, to an expectation of price-inflation. The conclusive evidence for this is what has happened to interest rates. If prices are expected to rise at 3 per cent per annum, an 8 per cent interest rate is no more burdensome to the borrower, and no more attractive to the lender, than a 5 per cent interest rate would have been, in conditions of stable prices. This is precisely the way in which rates of interest, in many countries, have adjusted. In the old days of fairly stable prices, a 7 per cent Bank Rate was a danger signal; now it is very comfortable (even, one might venture to suggest, rather low[1]).

One must, however, beware of taking such expectations too arithmetically. It is not just the case that people used to think that the price-level would be stable; now they expect it to rise at 3 (or 5) per cent per annum. If there was a *particular* expectation of rising prices, a firm expectation that prices would rise just so much and no further, it would act as a re-straining influence on the rises in costs that were felt to be tolerable, so it would do something (at least) to prevent that rate of price-rise being exceeded. Doubtless there is some-thing of this that remains; larger increases in selling prices are felt to be more dangerous than smaller; but the restraint that arises from this cause is very weak. There is an expectation

[1] $7 - 5 = 2$.

of rising prices, but it is an uncertain expectation.

Because it is uncertain, it is sensitive. Though (as experience shows) it is perfectly possible for people to become accustomed to a moderate rise in prices, continuing at much the same rate over long periods, nevertheless if anything happens to cause the price-rise to accelerate (even temporarily) the expectation of inflation lights up, and then becomes an independent cause of further inflation.

In this diagnosis, one is going along with the monetarists (such as Professor Milton Friedman and his associates). One can indeed have much sympathy with them in their desire to find a firmer basis for price-expectations. It is highly desirable that there should be some confidence in the movement of prices that is to be expected, within the period of time for which most business undertakings are planned. One may nevertheless have doubts about the means by which they seek to attain an end with which one agrees.

One can accept that in a world in which monetary stability (in some sense) was maintained, and was maintained long enough for people to feel condifence in its continuance, there would be some Quantity of Money which would adjust itself, or have to be adjusted, to this situation—changing (probably increasing) in a fairly regular fashion. (Just how this Quantity of Money should be measured is another matter; it might have to be measured in different ways in countries with different monetary institutions.) But it is quite a different thing to assert that control of the Quantity of Money, so as to make it behave in the way it would behave once that stability was established, would be a *sufficient* condition to ensure the attainment of that stability. The stability that is sought is a psychological condition, not to be achieved by such mechanical means, certainly not by them alone.

I can indeed imagine a world in which businessmen (and Trade Unionists) were so deeply imbued with Professor Friedman's principles that from a declared policy of regularity in the control of the Quantity of Money they drew the

consequences he desires them to draw; and in which governments (or perhaps a banking system independent of
government) were similarly dedicated; such a world, it is very
possible, would behave in the way he would like it to behave.
But I do not think it is our world, certainly not the part on
this side of the Atlantic. The restoration of monetary stability,
and of confidence in monetary stability, must in our world be
a much more complicated operation.

There is another question, of great interest and possible
future importance, that has been raised by Professor
Friedman.[2] What is the nature of the monetary stability at
which we should be aiming? Should we be aiming at constant
prices at gently falling prices, or at prices that are rising at
some moderate, but not excessive, rate? Whichever of these
objectives is chosen, it will be difficult enough to achieve it.
But one can hardly hope to begin, unless one has some idea of
what one wants to achieve.

The traditional meaning of monetary stability was constant
prices. The objective of monetary policy, we used to learn (in
the pre-Keynesian days when these things were accepted to
have the importance they are now recovering) was constancy
in the value of money. But if one asked why it is desirable
that the value of money should be constant, the principal
answer given was security of contract. 'Our economic order',
wrote Dennis Robertson,[3] 'is largely based on the institution
of contract—on the fact, that is, that people enter into voluntary but binding agreements with one another to perform
certain actions at a future date, for a remuneration that is
fixed here and now in terms of money. A violent or prolonged
change in the value of money saps the confidence with which
people make or accept undertakings of this nature.' This is an
important argument, which must be respected. But it is not in

[2] In his book, *The Optimum Quantity of Money* (1969).
[3] D. H. Robertson, *Money* (1928 edition), p. 13.

itself an argument for constancy. It is an argument for stability and reliability. If people are accustomed to a rise in prices at 3 per cent per annum, and they have confidence that that is approximately what will continue, they can adjust their contracts accordingly. We have seen them doing it. So when it is a question of choosing between one sort of stability and another, the old argument about security of contract does not much help.

Does it in fact make any difference to the working of an economy whether the value of money is constant or whether it is falling, so long as it is falling at a rate which is fully expected, and fully allowed for? If one is thoroughgoing in one's assumption of perfect adjustment, it is quite hard to see that there is. If the inflation is really fully allowed for, it does not itself seem to matter.

There is indeed only one reason, which has occurred to economists, why lesser inflation should be preferable to greater, even on this stringent test. I cannot, for my part, regard it as a very compelling reason, so long as the rate of inflation is moderate. It does indeed happen, in extreme inflations, that the loss of value from holding the depreciating money becomes a major consideration; when people receive money, they seek to pass it on as quickly as possible. Money loses its function as a store of value; so people are driven to satisfy their needs for 'convenience and security' in other ways, by holding their resources in what must inevitably be less convenient forms. One may grant that this would happen, in extreme inflation, even if the fall in the value of money was quite correctly foreseen. And one may grant that the loss which is imposed is a genuine loss, certainly a loss in 'welfare', and quite probably a loss that will reflect itself, to some extent, on the volume of production. If the want for 'convenience' has to be satisfied in more cumbrous ways, there will be costs of doing so; people will be spending their time in an unproductive activity, which could have been avoided.

There is no doubt that in major inflations this has happened; and that it has then been important. But it is hard to be convinced (even after studying Professor Friedman's econometrics) that in milder inflations, when there is no question of a 'flight from the currency', it is of much significance. It simply does not strike one as a compelling reason for preferring inflation at 3 per cent to inflation at 5 per cent per annum. Yet I believe that there is such a reason; but it is partly (at least) of a different character.

It is correct, nowadays, to take it that inflation is expected; but is is a mistake to suppose that the expectation is consistent. There is a schizophrenia about inflation. While in part of their behaviour (their investment behaviour, in particular) people show themselves to be inflation-minded, in the rest of it they go on as if they expected prices to be stable. The habits—business habits as well as personal habits—which are based on the assumption of stable prices are too strong to be easily broken. Nor is it just habits (like the division of housekeeping money within the family, one of the most intimate points at which—we have been learning—accelerated inflation hurts); it is also institutions. The accounting system, the tax system, even the general legal system, all are based on the assumption of a stable value of money; if the value of money is seriously changeable, they are twisted out of shape. The accountant's 'profits' cease to be true profits; the taxes that are imposed are different to what was intended; the fines and penalties imposed by the courts, as well as the compensations which they award, lose their proper effect. Now it is of course true that these things can be put right (for a time) by legislation; but only by re-opening issues that had been taken to be closed. There is waste of time in re-discussing them—surely a much more serious waste of time and energy than is involved in holding 'too small' money balances.

One must distinguish between the effects of inflation on different kinds of markets, different kinds of dealings. A 'perfect' competitive market, such as economists delight to use in their models, need be very little damaged by inflation. Dealers on such markets can allow for inflationary expectations in every transaction they make. The only real loss which accrues in that case is Friedman's loss—the loss of 'convenience and security' from the expected fall in the real value of money balances. But the only actual markets which approximate to this type are the financial markets; there, as we have seen, the allowance can be made, and in fact is made. It is not so simple a matter with the 'imperfect' markets, which are typical of the rest of the economy. In imperfect markets prices have to be 'made'; they are not just 'determined' by demand and supply. It is much easier to make them, in a way which seems satisfactory (because it seems fair) to the parties concerned, if substantial use can be made of precedent; if one can start with the supposition that what was acceptable befor will be acceptable again. When prices in general are fairly stable, that is often rather easy. The particular prices which result from such bargains may not be 'ideal' from the point of view of the economist; but the time and trouble which would be involved in 'improving' them is simply not worth while. To be obliged to make them anew, and to go on making them anew, as one is obliged to do in continuous inflation, involves loss—direct economic loss, and (very often) loss of temper as well.

It is of course in the labour market that such considerations are of particular importance; but it is by no means only to the labour market that they apply. Any system of prices (a system of railway fares, just like a system of wage-rates) has to satisfy canons of economic efficiency and canons of fairness—canons which it is very difficult to make compatible. It is bound to work more easily if it is allowed to acquire, in some degree, the sanction of custom—if it is not, at frequent intervals, being torn up by the roots.

This, I believe, is the principal reason why it is desirable that the rate of inflation, even if steady, even if 'expected', should be kept very modest. It is not necessarily conclusive against very modest rates of price-rise (say 2 or 3 per cent per annum); though one would expect that the economic and social conditions of different countries would give them, from this point of view, different margins of tolerance. One can even accept that a low rate of inflation may actually, sometimes at least, have advantages—making it, for instance, easier to bring about changes in relative wages (which may be desirable from the point of view of efficiency) without actually involving anyone in a reduction in his money wage. But this advantage, so far as it is an advantage, is itself dependent on some confidence in the value of money; so it is only at low degrees of inflation that it can be significant. As the inflation becomes more perceptible, it must be outweighed by the consequences just described.

It is these—the loss of time and temper in the continual revision of institutional, and quasi-institutional, arrangements—which are the principal charge to be brought against inflation, at the rate of inflation we are at present experiencing. Labour unrest is the leading but not the only example. The inconvenience which results, even in the financial markets, from loss of confidence in money as a store of value is surely, in this zone, a relatively minor matter.

I would however accept that there is something analogous to this loss of confidence which even today is already perceptible. It is possible that Friedman might choose to regard it as a special case of his effect—though it is an effect of inflation on 'imperfect' markets. It seems to me to be much less important than the effects I have just described; but it should not be omitted.

If one examines the balance-sheet of a business 'at a moment of time' it will usually be found to have among its assets not only some money which is not earning interest, but also some debts owing to it on which it is not charging interest. If one asks why it should hold assets in this latter form, the answer is surely that it is a matter of convenience, just like the reason for holding money. A debt that is due from a regular customer is not regarded in isolation; it is part of the regular relation between customer and supplier, which it is to the interest of both to maintain in a way that is convenient to both. On this, as on the money holding, inflation exercises a pressure. When money rates of interest are high (as we have seen they must be *in steady* inflation) the loss of interest that is involved in unpaid debts becomes more serious. It thus becomes profitable to take more trouble in collecting debts promptly, exerting pressure on debtors which would otherwise not need to be exerted. There is a real loss, measurable in labour-time, in exerting such pressure. And since the debtor himself has a similar incentive to delay payment, it is easily intelligible that the loss can be considerable.

We are accustomed to thinking of a credit squeeze as a temporary measure, designed to check or to reduce the rate of inflation. But this seems to show that if inflation is to be kept *steady*, at a rate that is more than very moderate, something in the nature of a credit squeeze has got to be present, not exceptionally, but all the time.

V HAWTREY*

The purpose of this paper is to discuss some aspects of the work of a distinguished economist,[1] who played an important part in the revolution in monetary theory of the twenties and thirties, the revolution which, in most people's minds, is exclusively associated with the name of Keynes. That there were others, of his generation, such as Pigou and Robertson who were also to some extent associated with it, appears even from a reading of the *General Theory* (1936) itself; though in that work they appear as little more than sparring-partners. If, however, one goes back to the *Treatise on Money* (1930)—and it is essential, for a full understanding of the *General Theory*, to go back to the *Treatise*—one finds that the part which they play in the later work is played by Hawtrey. I maintain that it is from Hawtrey that the story begins (the English story, that is, for I put on one side, in this paper, what was happening in Sweden[2]).

Hawtrey's *Currency and Credit* was published in 1919; thus it antedates every one of the 'new' monetary writings of Keynes. It was the standard work on monetary theory that was used, during the twenties, in the Cambridge Tripos;[3] thus it was natural than an important part of the *Treatise* should take the form of a reply to it. A reply to it, on the matters where Keynes and Hawtrey differed; I shall come to these in

* This is a slightly revised version of a paper which I gave to a conference in 1968, and which was printed under the title 'Automatists, Hawtreyans and Keynesians' in the *Journal of Money, Credit and Banking*, vol. 1 No. 3 (August 1969). pp. 307–17. Copyright © 1969 by the Ohio State University Press. All rights reserved.
[1] Sir Ralph Hawtrey died in 1975 at the age of 93. His long career in the British Civil Service (Treasury) began in 1904.
[2] See the section on Wicksell (and Myrdal) in Essay III above.
[3] As I am assured by Austin Robinson.

a moment, but only after insisting that on the most basic issue they were on the same side. When the chrysalis burst, and the debate (which in these formative years was confined to England) became worldwide, the doctrine that a free market system is not automatically self-righting was a chief stone of stumbling. To judge by many of the bright new books one reads, it still is. To those who come to the 'New Economics' only through the *General Theory* and the works that have followed it, the 'instability of capitalism' (the *monetary* instability) is a typically Keynesian doctrine; to some of them it is *the* characteristically Keynesian doctrine; the fact remains, however, that it is not specifically Keynesian at all. It has never been better stated than in the first chapter of *Currency and Credit*, the chapter with the provocative title 'Credit without Money'. Hawtrey starts straight off with a pure credit system, in which the media of exchange are simply debts (or credits); the banker is just a dealer in debts. Debts must be expressed in terms of a unit of account; but there is nothing to determine the value of the unit of account, save the carryover of memory, which makes people determine today's actions on the basis of yesterday's prices. And this, as he shows, though it prevents prices moving altogether erratically, does not prevent a continual slide in one direction or the other.

I shall not allow myself to be drawn into a discussion of the attempts to elude this key principle, which have gone on being made from that day to this. I shall merely state, rather baldly, the reason why I hold that they must be rejected. It is true that any general movement of prices involves a transference of real purchasing power from debtors to creditors, or from creditors to debtors; and there is a presumption, if one looks only at its effect on saving, that the transference will work in a stabilizing direction. But that is by no means the only force that must be taken into account. The 'wealth effect' has only been thought to be a sufficient stabilizer because the 'psychological' effect of the price-movement has been neglected. As soon as prices move sufficiently for people to extrapolate—to base their expectations of future prices not upon current prices but upon the way prices have been changing—a destabilizing force is set up which is bound to swamp the much weaker stabilizing power of the 'wealth effect'. That is the basic cause of the instability.

Though Hawtrey begins with the pure credit system, which has this inherent instability, he proceeds to modify it by introducing a 'hard money'—though only as one possible stabilizer. This, I am sure, is the right way to go about it. A free market economy does not have to have a hard money; and in fact, as time has gone on, the monetary system has approximated more and more closely to the pure credit system. The reasons for this have not been only, or even mainly, political. It is a natural development of the market economy—to substitute a cheaper means of payment for one which is more expensive; it will move in that direction if it is not stopped. And it is quite hard to stop it. Metallic money, in fact, has disappeared from internal circulation, and even in international transactions it is disappearing. The creation of a 'substitute hard money' by control over the quantity of some sort (or sorts) of money is continually defeated by human ingenuity in the invention of other sorts. Though (especially to begin with) they often seemed to slip back, Hawtrey and Keynes were surely right in holding that they were dealing with a system that had no automatic stabilizer: a system which needed to be stabilized by *policy*.

But by what policy? By what instruments of policy? We come now, of course, to the difference. It is a difference that has more aspects than are commonly noted. It will be useful to follow its history through, for it is quite instructive.

They started from common ground, not only on the need for policy, but in agreement that the instrument of policy was the rate of interest, or 'terms of credit', to be determined, directly or indirectly, by a Central Bank. But what rate of interest? It was Hawtrey's doctrine that the terms of bank lending had a direct effect on the activity of trade and industry; traders, having more to pay for credit, would seek to reduce their stocks, being therefore less willing to buy and more willing to sell. Keynes, from the start (or at least from the time of the *Treatise*—1930), rejected this in his opinion too simple view. He substituted for it (or began by substituting for it) an alternative mechanism through the long rate of interest. A change in the terms of bank lending affected the long rate of interest, the terms on which business could raise long-term capital; only in this roundabout way would a change in the terms of bank lending affect the activity of industry.

I think we can now see, after all that has happened, and has been said, since 1930, that the trouble with both of these views (as they were presented, or at least as they were got over) was that the forces they purported to identify were not strong enough to bear the weight that was put upon them. This is what Keynes said about Hawtrey (I quote from the *Treatise*):

The whole emphasis is placed on one particular kind of investment by dealers and middlemen in liquid goods—to which a degree of sensitivity to changes in Bank Rate is attributed which certainly does not exist in fact. . . . [He relies] exclusively on the increased costs of business resulting from dearer money. [He] admits that these additional costs will be too small materially to affect the manufacturer, but assumes without investigation that they do materially affect the trader. . . . Yet probably the question whether he is paying 5 or 6 per cent for the accommodation he receives from his banker influences the mind of the dealer very little more than it influences the mind of the manufacturer as compared with the current and prospective rate of take-off for the goods he deals in and his expectations as to their prospective price-movements. [*A Treatise on Money*, Vol. I, pp. 193–5.]

Granted, but could not very much the same be said of Keynes's own alternative mechanism? One has a feeling that in the years when he was designing the *General Theory* he was still clinging to it, for it is deeply embedded in the structure of his theory; yet one suspects that before the book left his hands it was already beginning to pass out. It has left a deep mark on the teaching of Keynesian economics, but a much less deep mark upon its practical influence. In the fight that ensued after the publication of the *General Theory*, it was quite clearly a casualty.

I suppose that in terms of influence upon the thinking of English economists (I am sorry to be so insular, even at a point where I ought not to be on my own principles, but I do not have the knowledge to go further) the turning-point was the publication in 1938 of the summary of replies to the Oxford questionnaire about the influence of the rate of interest on business decisions, to which 37 businessmen gave dusty answers.[4] But what to my mind is an even more effective demolition of the Keynesian mechanism came from Hawtrey himself.

It had taken him some time to mount his attack on Keynes's 'modus operandi of Bank Rate' but when it came it was formidable. The empirical data which Keynes had used to support his thesis were derived from a short period only— the 1920s; and Hawtrey was able to show that it was only in the first half of that decade (when, in the immediate aftermath of the War, the long rate in England was for that time unusually volatile) that an effect of monetary policy on the long rate, sufficient to give substantial support to Keynes's case, was at all readily detectable. Hawtrey took a much longer period. In *A Century of Bank Rate*[5] which, in spite of the narrowness of its subject, seems to me to be one of his best books—he ploughed through the whole of the British experience from 1844 to the date of writing; and of any effect of Bank Rate (or of any short rate) upon the long rate of interest, sufficient to carry the weight of Keynes's argument, he found little trace.

---

[4] P.W.S. Andrews and J.E. Meade, 'Summary of Replies to Questions on Effects of Interest Rates', *Oxford Economic Papers*, 1 (1938), 14–31.
[5] London: Longmans Green, 1939.

On the whole I think that we may infer that Bank Rate and measures of credit restriction taken together rarely, if ever, affected the price of Consols by more than two or three points; whereas a variation of one-eighth per cent in the long-term rate of interest would correspond to about four points in the price of a 3 per cent stock.

Now a variation of even less than one-eighth per cent in the long-term rate of interest ought, theoretically and in the long run, to have a definite effect for what it is worth on the volume of capital outlay. . . . But there is in reality no *close* adjustment of prospective yield to the rate of interest. Most of the industrial projects offered for exploitation at any time promise yields ever so far above the rate of interest. . . . [They will not be adopted until] promoters are satisfied that the projects they take up will yield a commensurate profit, and the rate of interest calculated on money raised will probably be no more than a very moderate deduction from this profit. [*A Century of Bank Rate*, pp. 170-1.]

There was a lot of guesswork and what would now seem to be very amateurish econometrics in all this; but the negative argument (in each case) was found convincing. Tweedledum and Tweedledee had both fallen flat, and the way was cleared for the Age of Fiscal Policy.

Hawtrey, however, would not admit that that is the end of the story, and I am inclined to agree with him. I think that there is something that survives. I would like to try to follow it out.

A Century of Bank Rate was largely concerned with the demolition of Keynes's method; but it also contains a restatement of Hawtrey's positive view. When I reviewed the book[6] I treated the points which he made on this side as 'new qualifications' which 'made the theory more acceptable'; Hawtrey refused to accept this description, insisting that they had been there all the time. It is indeed the case that there are references to them in his earlier works (as he stated in the *Reply*

[6] 'Mr. Hawtrey on Bank Rate and the Long-term Rate of Interest', *Manchester School of Economic and Social Studies*, 10 (1939), 21-37.

which he made to my review[7]; but I still do not feel that he had previously given them the same emphasis. They had not got over to me, and in this I am sure that I had plenty of company; it is clear, to take the leading example, that they had not got over to Keynes himself.

They are to be found in a section entitled 'Psychological Reactions' [*A Century of Bank Rate*, pp. 249 ff.]. I would rather doubt that the second point which he makes in that section is properly so described: it is a reminder of the imperfection of the loan market, a denunciation of the usual economist's fallacy of supposing that lenders are willing to lend indefinite amounts at a given rate of interest, so that the decision how much to borrow is made wholly by the borrower. This is perfectly valid, and perfectly relevant; but it is hardly necessary (now) to enlarge upon it. Perhaps I may cut it out, and leave what was said on the first point in isolation.

The pressure applied to traders by a moderate rise in the short-term rate of interest, say 1 per cent., is undeniably very slight. Yet apparently the Bank of England always counted on a rise of 1 per cent. or even ½ per cent. having a noticeable effect. . . . The explanation is. . . [that] when the use of Bank Rate to restrict credit became an established practice, traders, being aware of the intentions of the Bank, were inclined to anticipate them. When Bank Rate went up from 3 to 4 per cent., a trader would reason that this was intended to have a restrictive effect on markets, and that, if the effect was not brought about, the rate would simply go higher and higher until it was. . . . Those who took this view would restrict their purchases and demand would fall off, and so the 4 per cent. rate might be found potent enough, even though, if unsupported by traders' anticipations, a 6 or 7 per cent. rate might have been necessary. . . .

If the efficiency of Bank Rate depended upon these psychological reactions it would be precarious; for it people

[7] Hawtrey, 'Interest and Bank Rate', ibid. 144–56.

ceased to believe in it, the reactions would no longer occur. But the psychological reactions are in reality no more than a reinforcement of a tendency which in any case exists. Were they absent, that would only mean that Bank Rate would have to be raised higher. [Ibid., pp. 279 ff.]

As you will observe, Hawtrey in this book (and often indeed in his other works) is writing as an economic historian; he is analysing the working of a system of control which he holds to have operated at a particular place and time, a time which when he wrote must already have been, at least to some extent, in the past. This historical reference has probably limited the impact of what he wrote; but I think that it is a pity that it should have done so. For his particular system is also a standard system; it is a model of a working system of monetary control. That it is a model that can be used for the interpretation of a particular set of historical data is a source of strength. It puts it into a different class from many of our theoretical models.

But to have emphasized the historical application to such an extent, in the exposition of the theory, may well have been unfortunate; for it distracted attention from its *general* significance. Too much attention was in consequence concentrated upon the apparent implication that the principal channel by which Bank Rate exercises an effect is through its influence on the holding of stocks by traders. It is certainly true that Hawtrey was thinking (and in his historical application rightly thinking) of an economy in which the operations of traders upon rather perfect markets (including, in many cases, futures markets) occupied a key position; so that a change in the willingness of such traders to hold stocks would have effects on industry which radiated far and wide. We can recognize that it is in such an economy that the working of the Hawtrey system is at its most elegant. It is indeed an elegant type of economy; it survives for its elegance in many of our textbooks. But it is no longer a realistic description of an existing economy. Even in the thirties, at the time of the Keynes-Hawtrey controversy, it had already passed into history.

I am sure that Keynes was right in holding that he was dealing with an economy in which changes in the propensity to undertake fixed capital investment were more important, as a cause of fluctuation, than changes in the willingness to hold stocks. But it does not follow from this that a direct operation upon the decision *whether or not* to undertake fixed capital investment (the kind of effect which Keynes—at least in his first phase—thought to be capable of being exercised through the long rate of interest) is a convenient, or even a practicable, way of exercising control. Even in the case of fixed capital investment, even allowing for all the planning rigidities of which so much is made nowadays, it is possible for monetary control to be exercised over timing. Plans may interlock; the efficient execution of a development programme may require that its various sub-processes keep step with one another; yet the relation between plan time and calendar time remains to some extent elastic. And there are few expansion plans, even though they are to be mainly financed from retained profits, or from long-term capital raised upon the market, which do not depend upon the availability of bank credit *at some stage of the process*. The availability of bank credit, at such a stage, can still affect timing. It is his sense of the importance of timing which is expressed, in Hawtrey's model, by his emphasis on the *short-term* rate of interest. But the short-rate itself, though a symptom, is not the cutting edge; that is a matter of the availability of credit and the effect on expectations.

When I reviewed the *General Theory*, the explicit introduction of expectations was one of the things which I praised; but I have since come to feel that what Keynes gave with one hand, he took away with the other. Expectations do appear in the *General Theory*, but (in the main) they appear as *data*; as autonomous influences that come in from outside, not as elements that are moulded in the course of the process that is being analysed. Perhaps it is that famous (but I now think rather wicked) chapter on 'Long-term Expectations' which is the root of the trouble. For one can grant that there exists an

irrational element in expectations (the element of which
Keynes made so much) without conceding that they are so
irrational as to be random—and therefore incapable of being
moulded, at least to some extent, by policy.

I would maintain that in this respect Hawtrey is distinctly
superior. In his analysis of the 'psychological effect' of Bank
Rate—it is not just a vague indication, it is analysis—he identi-
fies an element which ought to come into any monetary
theory, whether the mechanism with which it is concerned is
Hawtrey's, or any other. I am indeed proposing, before I have
done, to suggest that it has a much wider significance. But
before I come to that, I must add a few further words on the
Hawtrey mechanism.

What is essential, on Hawtrey's analysis, is that it should be
possible (and should look as if it were possible) for the Central
Bank to take *decisive* action. There is a world of difference
(it follows from what he is saying) between action which is
determinedly directed to imposing restraint, so that it gives
the impression that if not effective in itself, it will be followed
by further doses of the same medicine; and identically the
same action which does not engender the same expectations.
Identically the same action may be *indecisive*, if it appears to
be no more than an adjustment to existing market conditions;
or if the impression is given that it is the most that is politically possible. If conditions are such that gentle pressure can
be exerted in a decisive manner, no more than gentle pressure
will as a rule be required. But as soon as there is doubt about
decisiveness, gentle pressure is useless; even what would otherwise be regarded as violent action may then be ineffective.
From this point of view (coming back to the historical application) the nationalization of the Bank of England was a
death-blow to the Hawtrey system. It was presented as making
little difference, but it did in fact make a great difference; for
it made the Bank constitutionally incapable of arousing the
expectations on which it had hitherto relied. If decisive action
was thereafter possible, it was only possible in crisis; the

gentler action which would have forestalled the crisis was prevented from having effect.

That, I believe, is indeed a part of the truth; but it is not a point that should be allowed to stand alone. The very notice-able tendency to a fall in the amplitude of the movements of Bank Rate between 1844 and 1875 on the one hand and 1875 to 1914 on the other can be explained, in Hawtrey's manner, as a sign that the market was 'learning'; but it can also be interpreted as a consequence of the growth of the inter-national capital market, which gave the Bank less freedom to operate an interest rate policy, the possibilities of which were closely circumscribed by international repercussions. The Bank was already ceasing to be a 'Monetary Authority' in the economist's sense; it was becoming no more than a Member Bank in an international system. This is recognized, of course, both by Keynes and by Hawtrey. It is presumably one of the reasons which led Keynes to turn towards Fiscal Policy, as being a method of control over which the single national government can have a freer hand. Hawtrey, I think one can see, came to favour the other way out. It is the fixed rate of exchange which imposes the international constraint; if that is abandoned, the Bank can recover its authority. A system in which the rate of exchange is free to move, while internal stability is maintained by a relentless application of the Bank Rate mechanism, is theoretically conceivable, and as a model it is instructive. But it would seem to depend for its working upon the maintenance of confidence in some *normal* rate of exchange, from which the current rate would be supposed to diverge only more or less temporarily; and it is not easy to see how such confidence could be engendered.

If only that obstacle could be overcome, one could see the Hawtrey mechanism working—and working, it is important to notice, *both ways*. For the Hawtrey system (especially when it is amended in this manner) is less affected than the Keynesian by the famous trouble of the 'floor' to the rate of interest: a trouble which is one of the legacies to 'modern' Keynesian economics of Keynes's preoccupation with the long rate, which (as we have seen) must be rejected, on other grounds, as an adequate stabilizer. In Hawtrey's (amended) model, high bank rate would be accompanied by a rise in the exchange above normal, which would reinforce the effect of the high bank rate on activity, and would also be a deterrent to the inflow of capital; since such capital, although it would earn a high rate of interest in the local money, would have to anticipate the probability of a loss on the exchange. Vice versa in the opposite case. The effect of low bank rate would be intensified by the downward fluctuation of the exchange (again supposed temporary). If confidence in the *normal* level of exchange could be maintained, this could work.

But it is not for the sake of this particular recipe (in which, as will be seen, I do not share Hawtrey's confidence) that I have been bringing you to retrace the steps of this old controversy. The moral I would draw from it myself is distinctly different.

I am certainly not contending that it is either possible, or desirable, that the Old King—Bank Rate—should be put back on his throne. We are living in the reign of his successor—the Government's Budget; that must be accepted. But the new reign, like the old, may not last for ever; we can already see that the storm clouds are gathering round it. Doubtless it has merits that the old did not have; but it has parted with some of the merits of the old. Is it quite impossible that they could, to some extent, be reincorporated?

There is a term which was invented, and then spoiled, by Pigou in his book on Public Finance,[8] on which I am itching to get my hand; it is the term *announcement effect*. I do not want to use it in the way Pigou did, but in a way which seems to me to be more appropriate. I want to use the announcement effect of an act of policy to mean the change which takes place in people's minds, the change in the prospect which they think to be before them, before there is any change which expresses itself in transactions of any kind. It is

[8] A.C. Pigou, *A Study of Public Finance* (London: Macmillan, 1928).

the same as what Hawtrey calls 'psychological effect'; but that is a bad term, for it suggests something irrational, and this is entirely rational. Expectations of the future (entirely rational expectations) are based upon the data that are available in the present. An act of policy (if it is what I have called a *decisive* action) is a significant addition to the data that are available; it should result, and should almost immediately result, in a shift in expectations. This is what *I* mean by an announcement effect.

What I learn from Hawtrey's analysis is that the 'classical' Bank Rate system was strong, or could be strong, in its announcement effects. Fiscal policy, at least as so far practised, gets from this point of view much worse marks. It is not simply that it is slow, being subject to all sorts of parliamentary and administrative delays; made indecisive, merely because the gap between announcement and effective operation is liable to be so long. This is by no means its only defect. Its announcement effect is poor, for the very reason which is often claimed to be one of its merits—its selectivity; for selectivity implies complexity and an instrument which is to have a strong announcement effect should, above all, be simple. That fiscal policy is inefficient as a signal has long been recognized; it is one of the reasons for the rise of 'indicative planning'. But a Plan, even more than a budget, is too cumbrous to be an effective signal. It is announced that the Plan is to be revised. How? We have to wait and see.

I am nevertheless by no means inclined to argue that Bank Rate, or its equivalent, is the only possible signal that can have a fair degree of announcement efficiency. I feel sure that we should be looking about for possible alternatives.

There was a time, in England in the 1950s, when it appeared to be possible that the standard rate of income tax might be used as a Regulator; it would have been less efficient than the 'classical' Bank Rate, but is is conceivable that up to a point it might have worked. Income tax, however, has a distributional function which is properly regarded as paramount. This has caused it to move away, first from a flat rate,

and then from a schedule that is dominated by a single parameter—towards a schedule that is subject to continual tinker-
ing, in which the possibility of simple *decisive* movement gets
lost. In this field, again, selectivity has been the enemy of
announcement efficiency.

Corporation tax which in England dates from 1965 is
imposed at a flat rate; it could therefore be used for the
purpose that I have in mind, and there have been indications
that it is intended so to use it. Yet at much the same time as
the Wilson Government introduced the corporation tax, which
could have this advantage, they threw away the old system of
flat rate investment allowances, a means of control which was
quite promising in its announcement effect; substituting for it
a selective system of investment grants, so arbitrary and uncertain in its operation that the possibility of using it to get
an announcement effect is almost zero. But perhaps it is
possible that some day England will revert to the former
system of investment allowance; the opportunity of using
Corporation Tax as a regulator would then be much better.

It is hard to see that indirect taxation, however general
(such as might be levied through a universal sales tax, or value
added tax, or employment tax), could ever have a high degree
of announcement efficiency. It is condemned by the perver-
sity of its effect on anticipations. As soon as an upward movement of the tax rate is anticipated, there will be an incentive
to try to beat the gun, and vice versa the other way. I do not
mean that these devices may not have some part to play, but
it is hard to see that they could be usable as a principal
instrument.

The rate of interest—the short rate of interest—when
properly interpreted as a symbol of credit ease or credit
stringency, has a superiority over all tax methods, in that it
gets the timing of its announcement effects just what they
should be. If it cannot be used in the 'classical' way, we should
be on the look-out for new ways in which it could be used.

One, which would possibly seem to be worth exploring,
would be to use it for the regulation of the investment

expenditure of the Public Sector itself. In the Hawtrey model, the direct impact of Bank Rate was on the holding of stocks by dealers, taken to be a key sector of the economy. An efficient Regulator must operate directly upon some key sector; the investment expenditure of the Public Sector, in the semi-socialized economies which have now become the rule, would seem to be a promising candidate. If public bodies (in the British case, local authorities, nationalized industries, and other supported institutions—such as universities!) were obliged to finance their investment expenditure by loans from a government bank, that Bank could finance them at a rate of interest which was variable, and which need have no regular relation with rates of interest on international markets. It could be raised as high as desired; and if desired it could be made negative. But the existence of this freedom of movement would mean (for Hawtrey's reason) that once the signal had been learnt, big swings should not be necessary. In view of the effect on expectations—not only within the Public Sector, but also outside it—moderate movements should suffice.

This, perhaps, is a dream; I do not claim to be a judge of political possibilities. But I am not afraid to draw the moral, which emerges rather clearly from the line of thought I have tried to follow out, that the issue with which we have been concerned is political—even constitutional—as well as economic. There is the technical economic problem of the Instrument; but it is tied up with the political problem of how to secure that it is used decisively. This is a problem which Keynesian economics, so it seems to me, has refused to face; while the monetarists, who have seen it, have not faced the political implications. For myself, I would face it. I think we should say that monetary regulation is a major function of Government; but we should emphasize that if it is to be exercised decisively, it needs to be separated, in what is in fact the constitutional sense, from other functions. We need to remember the ancient doctrine of the Separation of Powers. The judicial function, in well-ordered states, is recognized to be a function of Government, but a function that is better *separated*. So it is with the monetary function. It is far too responsible a function to be handed over to a 'company of merchants' (Ricardo's pejorative expression for the Bank of England). Nevertheless it is harmful for it to be confused, as Keynesianism has led it to be confused, with the regular financing of the executive government. It belongs to the province of the executive government to further the maintenance of high employment and steady growth, within the framework of an economy that is monetarily well-regulated. But it is a disaster that these things have got so mixed together.

VI RECOLLECTIONS AND DOCUMENTS*

This is the story of my personal 'Keynesian Revolution' which (though I was not a member of Keynes's circle) goes back before 1936. The route by which I got to some semi-Keynesian ideas, such as are expressed in my 'Suggestion for simplifying the theory of money' (written in 1934 and published in *Economica* in February 1935), may even now be of interest; for it is related to the tracks which have been followed by much more recent writers, Patinkin and Leijonhufvud, for instance. It has fortunately not been necessary for me to rely entirely upon deceitful memory, since there are documents (letters and so on) which have remained in my possession, so that I can use them, and shall use them, in the following.

I begin in the autumn of 1929. I was then a junior lecturer at L.S.E., having graduated from Oxford four years before. I thought of myself as a labour economist; I had already written some of the more applied part of my *Theory of Wages*. I had learnt very little general economics at Oxford;[1] but already in my first years at L.S.E. I was beginning to catch up. Yet at that point I knew nothing at all about Money; so when I read of the Stock Market crash I had no idea what it meant.

In October 1929 Lionel Robbins came to L.S.E. as professor; and then things began to hum. I had some mathematical

---

* A paper given to a meeting of the Money Study Group at Oxford in 1972, and printed in *Economica*, Feb. 1973. Reproduced by permission of the London School of Economics and Political Science.
[1] I took P.P.E. in the second year of its existence, when the necessary teaching was far from having taken shape. My tutor in economics was a military historian, who had no interest in the subject, and failed to awaken any in me. I turned to economics after I had taken my degree, through a fortunate contact I had with Graham Wallas, and through him with L.S.E.

training; so he moved me to lecturing on parts of economics where I could use my mathematics. The first fruits were a draft of what was to become the elasticity of substitution chapter in *Theory of Wages*, and a paper about Edgeworth and Marshall on the labour market, which appeared in the *Economic Journal* in June 1930. It was this latter which set me up as an economic theorist.

The subjects on which I was set to lecture were General Equilibrium (Walras and Pareto)—and Risk. The General Equilibrium lectures had their own consequences; most of that, however, is not relevant here.[2] It was through Risk that I got to Money.

Not indeed immediately. The first thing that came out of the Risk lectures was a paper 'The Theory of Uncertainty and Profit', which appeared in *Economica* in 1931. This must have been written already in 1930, since I have a letter from Keynes, dated December 1930, rejecting it for the *Economic Journal*. When I look at that letter now, I find it rather interesting. His main reason for rejecting it is clearly that he thinks I have had my turn—my Edgeworth paper had only just appeared—but he also thinks it is rather half-baked, as indeed it is. But he does *not* make the criticism which he surely would have made later—and which I myself should have made later—that I try to treat choice under uncertainty in terms of the current flow account, not in terms of the balance-sheet, as it should have been treated. Naturally enough, as long as I was doing that, I could not get across to Money.[3]

[2] *Theory of Wages* elasticity of substitution; Joan Robinson's elasticity of substitution (*Imperfect Competition*) 1933; proof of equivalence in two-factor case; Lerner's proof that the Robinson elasticity is a property of an isoquant; my own realization that the same geometrical property would hold for an indifference curve. Those are the steps that led to the Hicks–Allen article, which appeared in *Economica*, Feb. 1934.

[3] Still it was something (at that date) to have envisaged the risk problem as one of choice among probability distributions. And it is also of interest that economic probability distributions were considered to be (very often) inherently non-symmetric. (See Essay VIII below).

December 1930—the date of that letter—is the date of publication of the *Treatise on Money*. I suppose I read it, or some of it, when it appeared, but I must have read it quite uncomprehendingly. I was mainly occupied, during 1931, which finishing *Theory of Wages*, which had begun as applied Pigou (with a dash of Walras), but then got overlaid in its final stages with a coating of Hayek. For 1931 was the advent of Hayek at L.S.E.; even before he arrived as professor (in October), even before the *Prices and Production* lectures, which he gave as a visitor in the previous February, we were reading the 'Austrians'. The effect on my book, so far as capital theory is concerned, was (one can now see) by no means bad; but the innocent acceptance of 'neutral money' notions, in the few places where money is even mentioned,[4] is something of which very soon I was to become greatly ashamed.

I can't go further without Dennis Robertson. I first met him when he gave a paper at L.S.E. in the summer of 1930, but our real meeting was in Vienna in the following September—a quite casual meeting when I was on holiday; we went to the *Meistersinger* together. After that we never lost touch; it was most important to me to have someone to consult outside the L.S.E. circle. I have a pile of correspondence with him throughout these years and later; it is of much help to me in piecing the story together.

All of the first part of it relates to *Theory of Wages*. For it so happened that he was the reader whose advice on publication was sought by Macmillan. We were already good enough friends for that to have to come out! So he sent me some of his comments. He had said that he felt 'a good deal out of sympathy with the extravagant dogmatism of the stable from which it comes', but nevertheless felt that it ought to be published. 'Of course', he says in an accompanying letter, 'I think you've all gone dotty about capital decumulation; there's some excuse for Hayek, having lived in mouldering Vienna, but none for the rest of you, having lived in London and the

[4] Especially pp. 133-5.

Home Counties.' But we went on arguing about substitution (or variation) for quite a time.

Thus by mid-1932 I had *Theory of Wages* finished; and I went back to Risk. Almost at once something happened. The path on which I started was to lead to 'Simplifying the Theory of Money', but that was two years later. There are two earlier stages, which can be identified. The second was actually published, in German, in the *Zeitschrift für Nationalökonomie*, under the title 'Gleichgewicht und Konjunktur', in a number that is dated '4 of 1933', but which actually appeared in the summer of that year.[5] The first was never published, but I have a copy, with a comment on it by Dennis, dated November 30, 1932.

You may find it interesting if I read the first pages of this first draft—not the last part, which goes off the rails in a rather shameful manner, as Dennis of course pointed out. (This was corrected in the German version.)

The most fundamental doctrine in almost all modern theories of the Trade Cycle is that of 'the inherent instability of credit', which we, in this country, associate particulary with Mr. Hawtrey. I accept this doctrine; but I wish to point out thàt it is in all probability ònly a single case—though doubtless the most important case—of a much more general proposition. *The use of money is inconsistent with economic equilibrium.*

In practical application my generalization adds little directly to Mr. Hawtrey's, but I think it adds a good deal indirectly. For it suggests a new line of approach.

I must explain first that I use equilibrium in its most extended and most modern sense. The concept of equilibrium has undergone a long evolution since it was first made precise by Edgeworth's introduction of the notion of 're-contract'. It came then to refer to a market in which buyers and sellers continually bought and sold at the same prices, because no-one had any incentive to change. This was generalized for

[5] I had a suspicion of this from my correspondence; the fact has since been confirmed by Dr. Hennings.

the whole economic system (perhaps rather hastily) by Pareto.

Pareto's own system is inadequate because it pays too little attention to the obvious fact that men are influenced in their present actions by their expectations of future situations. A full equilibrium in the modern sense (as elaborated by Prof. Knight and, independently by Prof. Hayek) allows for the influence of future prices on action as well as present prices. [Knight, *Risk, Uncertainty and Profit*, Ch. 5; Hayek, 'Das intertemporale Gleichgewichtsystem', *Weltwirtschaftliches Archiv*, 1928.]

Further, this recent extension removes the necessity for the most unrealistic and uncomfortable assumptions of the Paretian system—the assumption that the economic data (tastes, knowledge, capital and so on) remain always the same. We can have equilibrium in a changing world. The condition for equilibrium is perfect foresight; men must always act in such a way that the prices (present and *future*) on which they base their actions, should actually be realized. Disequilibrium is the disappointment of expectations.

Now, of course, it is obvious that, owing to men's ignorance of future changes in the data (and still more owing to their ignorance of the consequences of changes, whether future, present or, perhaps, past) such perfect equilibrium can never be attained. Nevertheless, it is extremely helpful to be able to classify on one side those economic phenomena which are consistent with equilibrium—and to which, therefore, we can directly apply equilibrium analysis—and on the other those which are not. I believe that money goes into the second class.

Suppose we have a community which possesses a given volume of money (by which I mean simply currency) and for the sake of precision suppose that the money material has no 'industrial' use. Then it is necessary that at any moment the money should be divided among the individuals composing the community in proportion to their demand for it. But what governs their demand for it? Only their need to use it for making future payments. They do not need the money for making present payments—otherwise they would not be holding the money but paying it out. It is only for future payments that they need to hold it.

But now it must be observed that it is only for future

payments that are uncertain that it is absolutely necessary to hold money. If the date and amount of the future payments are absolutely certain, then there is no need to hold money against them—it will be more profitable to lend it until the future payment falls due. Such holding of money implies that the holder is doing something which is against his interest; and therefore the position is not one of equilibrium.

It may be objected that this drastic conclusion implies that people can find profitable uses for money available for the shortest conceivable period; but the answer surely is, they do. They lend it out through a middleman—the banker. [Cf. Wicksell on the 'virtual velocity of circulation', *Vorlesungen*, II.]

Nor can the further objection be admitted (though I confess that it impressed me for a little) that the time taken by actual payments sets an irreducible minimum to the social demand for money. The bank cheque and the bill of exchange are hoary devices for overcoming precisely this difficulty.

I maintain, therefore, that if people foresee perfectly the future course of economic data and the consequent course of prices, they will have no demand to hold money at all. They will dispose of all their money on loan—either through the instrumentality of the banks or through some other equivalent mechanism. Under the same assumptions, it is evident that the banker will need to keep no cash reserve.

If no stocks of money are being kept, the level of prices (though, of course, not the ratios of the prices) is altogether indeterminate. On the other hand, if stocks are being kept, the situation is not one of equilibrium; since it will always be to the interest of any individual to increase his own future income at no sacrifice whatever by lending out his stock.

If we accept this argument, then (on a lower plane of refinement) these conclusions seem to follow:

1. Save as a methodological abstraction (and a very dangerous abstraction, since it runs counter to most ordinary theoretical assumptions) there is no such thing as a 'neutral money'.

2. It is no use blaming disequilibrium on the banks; still less, to attribute it to banking monopoly and call for 'Bankfreiheit'. Banking monopoly is the only thing which holds out any hope of maintaining a semblance of equilibrium in an advanced economy.

3. The velocity of circulation of money is fundamentally a function (an inverse function) of risk. Habit and the distribution of habits may obscure this; but only in the same way as they obscure other economic tendencies. The generalization of Mr. Hawtrey's doctrine gives us a Risk Theory of Money.

4. The trade cycle is a monetary phenomenon in this sense only; that any large unexpected change in the economic data must influence the risk factor and therefore the velocity of circulation of money. Every large change must produce one causal sequence through its monetary repercussions; whatever be the *causa causans* of the trade cycle, it must have a significant monetary aspect.

When the risk factor is present, it will have an extremely significant influence on the way in which a man holds his assets. In times of utter chaos and mutual distrust, he will desire to hold all his assets in the form of immediately disposable purchasing power, i.e. of money. With rather greater confidence, he will be prepared to hold some in rather less disposable forms. In times of great confidence considerable parts of his assets will be locked up in forms not at all immediately available—because he does not take at all seriously the chance that they will not be available if he should happen to want them.

In advanced communities, a representative individual may be considered as holding his assets in innumerable different forms, which however may be broadly classified:

Cash, call loans, short loans, long loans, material property with shares).

Broadly speaking, there is an increasing risk element as we go from left to right. And, again, broadly speaking, there is a higher promise of return in the same direction to compensate for the increased risk. The distribution of his assets among these forms is governed by the relative promise of return and by the relative risk factor. . . .

I had written that before the end of 1932. In spite of its crudity (and obvious mistakes), there are things which can be claimed for it. I was by that time thinking in terms of the balance-sheet; I had got to the 'spectrum of assets'. And I had drawn some (though by no means all) of the consequences.

There is nothing about Keynes in this first draft, but when I showed it to Barrett Whale, he said, 'That sounds like the *Treatise on Money*'. So at that point (but not earlier) I did go to the *Treatise*, a reference to which is made in the German paper. And when the German paper appeared, I thought I might send it (the English original of it) to Keynes. At this time (August 1933) he had no doubt been reading Shove's review of *Theory of Wages*, which appeared in the *Journal* in September 1933 and had of course passed through his hands; so he was thinking of me as committed to the 'dogmatism of the L.S.E. stable'. But he says:

as you suppose, there is a good deal with which I do not agree, but it is now clear that our minds are no longer moving in opposite directions. In the last few weeks I think I have put my finger on the fundamental point which, quite apart from saving and investment decisions, separates me not only from you and Pigou but from everyone since Ricardo. But it is more than can be discussed in a letter.

I still don't know, at all precisely, what the 'point' was.[6]

It was a year after that that I wrote the third version—

---

[6] I do, however, know what was the point which, at that stage and for some time afterwards, separated me from what was to become the 'economics of Keynes'. Like Pigou (and Dennis Robertson) I thought that we were talking about *fluctuations*—booms and slumps, which, since they did not rest in complete collapse or complete explosion, could not have engendered a universal expectation of going on for ever. Booms could then be considered to be times of high prices, slumps as times of low prices—with regard to some norm, which throughout the fluctuations would be unchanged, or not much changed. (In the terminology of *Value and Capital*, expectations were inelastic, fairly inelastic.) Keynes, with his keen nose for the actual, the current actual, sensed that in the Great Depression, during which we were then living, that was ceasing to be true; I am sure he was right in thinking that it was ceasing to be true. It is quite another matter whether he was right to project his vision on to so wide a canvas. Later experience has indicated that the formation of expectations is a more complicated matter and a more tricky matter, than could have been envisaged by anyone— Keynesians, anti-Keysians, or semi-Keynesians—in 1930–6.

'Simplifying'.[7] When I sent that (in proof) to Keynes, I got this postcard, dated Dec. 24, 1934:

Many thanks for the proof of your article. I like it very much. I agree with you that what I now call 'Liquidity Preference' is the essential concept for Monetary Theory.

That was the first time I had heard of Liquidity Preference.

I should probably explain that up to this point I had never talked with Keynes. The first time I met him personally was when I was interviewed by him and Pigou, over lunch, for my appointment as University Lecturer at Cambridge. That must have been in May 1935. So it was after that he wrote me a note, dated June 1935, in which he says:

The channels[8] through which my ideas are reaching you sound rather alarming! Probably you will gather the tendency, but do not take the details too seriously! My book is a fairly fat one and I try to cover the whole ground of the fundamentals. But in my own view it is merely a beginning. I agree with you that very large vistas are opening up. I deliberately refrain in my forthcoming book from pursuing anything very far, my object being to press home as forcefully as possible certain fundamental opinions—and no more.

I knew no more of the details until I was asked, very much to my surprise, to review the *General Theory* for the *Economic Journal* (on its publication in January 1936).

It was no doubt because of 'Simplifying' that I had this difficult honour conferred upon me.[9] I was not a member of the Keynes's group; but I had shown in that paper that there

[7] 'A Suggestion for Simplifying the Theory of Money', *Economica*, Feb. 1935, (reprinted in *Critical Essays*).
[8] These no doubt were notes on the lectures that Keynes had been giving at Cambridge—notes which were beginning to circulate at L.S.E.
[9] I had just three months in which to write my review—January to April. It is therefore, in many ways, no more than a first impression.

were some ideas in the book which would be uncongenial to me. In fact there were more than could have been told from 'Simplifying'; for in the meantime I had been in touch with what was happening in Sweden.

It began with Myrdal's *Monetary Equilibrium*, which I read in German and reviewed in *Economica* (November 1934).[10] I found this most exciting, not so much for its positive conclusions (as I said in my review, I remained a little puzzled just what Monetary Equilibrium was for) as for the range of ideas which it opened up. The general method, the use of static analysis for the determination of a short-period macro-equilibrium, with expectations included as data—the method which Keynes was to use so brilliantly—I had already got from Myrdal. And I had more understanding of it than I got directly from Myrdal, because of a fortunate chance that brought me into contact with Erik Lindahl, who was in London for the summer of 1934 and again in 1935. The critical work, on which Myrdal's book was based, was largely due to Lindahl. He was the father of Social Accounting *theory*; it was lucky that when I came to reviewing Keynes, I had that behind me too.[11]

[10] The four works which were bound together as *Beiträge zur Geldtheorie*, Vienna, 1933, were jointly reviewed by J.C. Gilbert and myself. I took Fanno and Myrdal; he took Holtrop and J.C. Koopmans.

[11] It was for this reason that I laid such stress, in the first part of my review, on the introduction of the 'method of expectations'. What I meant was the introduction of expectations as explicit variables in a formal 'equilibrium' theory. That, perhaps, was not made clear enough. It caused much trouble to Dennis Robertson, who began an onslaught with a schoolboy joke 'Expectorans expectoravi' (see Psalm 40 in the Book of Common Prayer); and continued for months to bombard me with quotations from Marshall, Fisher, Lavington, and so on, to show that they *had* taken expectations into account. I laid myself open to this, by not fully perceiving that the issue was a matter of the status of Keynes's 'quasi-static' model, a model which Dennis rejected, as one feels sure it would have been rejected by the authorities he was quoting. He was right, one can now see, to perceive its weaknesses; but he was too much occupied with its weaknesses to perceive its strengths.

I have some correspondence with Keynes about that review—quite interesting in itself, but it would take too long to go into it here.[12] So I pass to what was in effect my second review: 'Mr Keynes and the Classics'. This appeared in *Econometrica* in 1937, but was originally given at a meeting of the Econometric Society in Oxford in September 1936. I expect you will find Keynes's comments on that the most interesting part of my collection, so I will give them in full. The letter is dated March 31, 1937.

At long last I have caught up with my reading and have been through the enclosed. I found it very interesting and really have next to nothing to say by way of criticism.

From one point of view you are perhaps scarcely fair to the classical view. For what you are giving is a representative belief of a period when economists had slipped away from the pure classical doctrine without knowing it and were in a much more confused state of mind than their predecessors had been. The story that you give is a very good account of the beliefs which, let us say, you and I used to hold. But if you were to go further back, how far back I am not sure, you would have found a school of thought which would have considered this an inconsistent hotch-potch. The inconsistency creeps in, I

[12] The chief points which arose were four. (1) My point about stocks, and the elasticity of supply of consumption goods—the principal point on which I had dissociated myself from a strict Keynesian position. Here Keynes was able to show that what I had said was incorrect *on his assumptions*. The point should have been made differently. I was nevertheless still convinced—and I remain convinced—that there was some substance in what I was saying. (2) The definition of income; here, with Lindahl behind me, I think I had the better of the argument. (3) Opposition, or equivalence, of monetary and loanable funds determination of interest rate. Here I was already thinking in terms of the *Value and Capital* 'week' model, which avoids the stock-flow confrontation. Having these assumptions of my own at the back of my mind, I was naturally unable to make my point convincingly. (4) Own-rates of interest, on which, towards the end of 1936, Keynes was already making considerable qualifications to what he had said in his book.

The correspondence is printed in Keynes, *Collected Writings*, Vol. XIV, pp. 70–81.

suggest, as soon as it comes to be generally agreed that the increase in the quantity of money is capable of increasing employment. A strictly brought up classical economist would not, I should say, admit that. We used formerly to admit it without realizing how inconsistent it was with our other premises.

On one point of detail. I regret that you use the symbol *I* for income. One has to choose, of course, between using it for income or investment. But, after trying both, I believe it is easier to use *Y* for income and *I* for investment. Anyhow we ought to try and keep uniform in usage.

On particular passages I have made the following notes:

1. On *page 4* you make saving a function of money income. This is all right so long as you assume wages constant. But after removing this assumption on page 5 it is no longer safe, I suggest, to regard saving as a function of money income.

2. Second complete paragraph on *page 5*. I agree that we probably slipped into thinking this. But a strict classical economist would say that an increase in the supply of money would only raise money incomes and not real incomes.

3. *Page 12*. Bottom paragraph. From my point of view it is important to insist that my remark is to the effect that an increase in the inducement to invest *need* not raise the rate of interest. I should agree that, unless the monetary policy is appropriate, it is quite likely to. In this respect I consider that the difference between myself and the classicals lies in the fact that they regard the rate of interest as a non-monetary phenomenon, so that an increase in the inducement to invest would raise the rate of interest irrespective of monetary policy—though they might concede that monetary policy was capable of producing a temporary evaporating effect.

4. *Page 17*. At one time I tried the equations, as you have done, with *I* in all of them. The objection to this is that it over-emphasizes *current* income. In the case of the inducement to invest, *expected* income for the period of the investment is the relevant variable. This I have attempted to take account of in the definition of the marginal efficiency of capital. As soon as the prospective yields have been determined, account has been implicitly taken of income, actual and expected. But, whilst it may be true that entrepreneurs

are over-influenced by present income, far too much stress is laid on this psychological influence, if present income is brought into such prominence. It is, of course, all a matter of degree. My own feeling is that present income has a predominant effect in determining liquidity preference and saving which it does not possess in its influence over the inducement to invest.[13]

I think I may conclude from this letter (as I have always done) that Keynes accepted the *ISLM* diagram as a fair statement of his position—of the nucleus, that is, of his position. That, in any case, was what it was meant to be—a means of demonstrating the nature of the difference between Keynes and his predecessors[14]—not a statement of what I believed myself.

It is much less a statement of my own view than the 'Simplifying' article, by which I continue to stand much more nearly. I have come to believe that what I was saying there is by no means the same as Keynes's Liquidity Preference doctrine, as Keynes (you will remember) thought at first that it was. Keynes's Liquidity Preference, with its simple substitution between Money and Bonds, is a much grosser simplification; it leaves out quite a lot of the problem.

I had discovered by the time of 'Simplifying': (1) that one

[13] Keynes's page references are a typescript of the article, now disappeared. But the passages to which he refers are fairly easily identified.

[14] Keynes was of course quite right to criticize my presentation of 'classical' theory. It was polite of him to suggest that what I gave was something which he himself had at one time believed; I much doubt it! For my part, I do have to plead guilty; for this was precisely the 'theory' to which I had committed myself in that dreadful passage of *Theory of Wages*. 'Classical' theory—whether in Keynes's sense, that in which Pigou and Robertson were 'classics', or in the conventional sense, of Ricardo and Mill and their contemporaries—was surely a great deal more subtle. But it also is capable of being illustrated, to the same extent as the Keynes theory is capable of being illustrated, on the *ISLM* diagram, when suitably adapted. This was shown in a paper, allegedly about Patinkin, which I published in the *Economic Journal* in 1957 and which is reprinted in a better form, as 'The "Classics" Again', in *Critical Essays in Monetary Theory* (1967).

has to work in terms of the balance-sheet; (2) that choice between assets is choice between probability distributions; (3) that the cost of making transactions is vital—so that uncertainty of the period for which the presently chosen balance-sheet will remain the optimum balance-sheet is one of the chief things that matters. I believe I had all these things by the end of 1934. There are traces of all of them in the *Treatise*, but in the *General Theory* Keynes has simplified so much that the third is pretty well left out. As a result, his Liquidity Preference is misnamed. It makes the demand for money depend on Uncertainty, not Liquidity. The Liquidity motive, properly so called (I used to say in lectures), is that which makes a cat leave the room when the door is opened, even if she has been quite comfortable inside. It is the vital consideration in the demand for liquid assets; but in the General Theory, where is it?

I am sure I had this distinction many years ago; but I did not write it out properly until the latter part of the second paper of my 'Two Triads'.[15] I think I still stand by what I said there, though it is still incomplete; there is more to be done.[16]

May I conclude with some remarks on how the Keynes theory appears to me now, in our present much longer perspective? We have to remember that the Keynesian Revolution was not just a revolution in economic theory. Keynes was a prophet, or propagandist; there were many audiences to which he was addressing himself. He was selling his policy to politicians and public, by *Essays in Persuasion* and by newspaper articles galore. The *General Theory* was his way of selling his policy to professional economists. It is tailored, most skilfully tailored, to their habit of mind. 'The technique of the book', as I said in my first review, 'is conservative'—that

[15] *Critical Essays*, pp. 30–6.
[16] Some more is done in the second section of my *Crisis in Keynesian Economics* (Blackwell, 1974).

is to say, it provides a model on which academic economists can comfortably perform their accustomed tricks. Haven't they just? With *ISLM* I myself fell into the trap. I should have been warned by that little note of June 1935 which I quoted earlier. For now, at greater distance, we find (I believe) that the *General Theory* loses stature, while the *Treatise*, in spite of its eccentricities, grows. The *General Theory* is a brilliant squeezing of dynamic economics into static habits of thought. The *Treatise* is more genuinely dynamic, and therefore more human.

VII CAPITAL CONTROVERSIES: ANCIENT AND MODERN*

In what must be a fairly short paper, it will not be expected that I should make a survey of all controversies about capital, from (say) Ricardo-Malthus to Joan Robinson-Solow. All I can attempt is something much more modest. What I propose to do is to take one particular point, which has figured (as I shall show) in many such controversies, and to use it as a means of pulling a part of the story together. It is an interesting illustration of the way in which the history of his subject can be of use to the modern economist.

Economists do indeed have a special use for the history of economics, something more than the general use that can be made of their own history by students of other subjects such as mathematics and the natural sciences. The history of science, certainly, is no mere antiquarianism; one is learning science when one learns in what ways scientific discoveries have been made. The history of economics has that use, and it has other uses. It has, of course, a pure historical use; the greatest economists, Smith or Marx or Keynes, have changed the course of history; they are as worthy the attention of the pure historian as Louis Napoleon or Woodrow Wilson. But this again is not the economist's use. That is something different.

Economics is a social science, and a particular kind of social science, in that it is concerned with the rational actions, the calculated actions, of human beings, and with their consequences. This has the result that those whom we study can hear what we say. We may speak to each other in our private languages, but private conversations are no more than goods in

* A paper given at a meeting of the American Economic Association in New York, and printed in the *American Economic Review* (May 1974). Reproduced by permission of the American Economic Association.

process; while we speak only to each other we have not finished our job. The ideas of economics, the powerful ideas of economics, come from the market-place, the 'real world', and to the 'real world' they go back. So there is a dialogue between economists and their subject-matter. It is a dialogue in which there are important intermediaries; statisticians are one kind of intermediary, journalists another, accountants (as we shall see) another; the economist-statistician and the economist-journalist do much of the intermediation themselves. In the course of the dialogue ideas acquire associations; they cease to be free ideas, which can be defined at choice. It is not in our power to say with Humpty-Dumpty, 'When I use a word it means just what I choose it to mean'; we cannot escape the associations.

I do not mean that there is not such dialogue, and such associations, in the case of other social sciences. Clearly there is; in political science, say, as much, if not more, than in economics. Political ideas are indeed so rich in associations that the study of politics seems sometimes to consist of little else. Economics has (relatively) much more that is positive to offer, but we should not allow our passion for quantification to blind us to the fact that economic ideas share this characteristic of political ideas and do so for the same reason.

We cannot escape the associations, but we can try to understand them, so as to be masters of them. That is what, in my view, the history of economics is for. It is what it is for, for the economist. We need to know the history of our concepts in order to know what it is that we are handling.

The history of economics, so understood, cannot be discovered by poring over old textbooks, even old 'classics'. That is no more than a part of what has to be done. The books must be read against their background, the events which prompted the analysis and what happened to the analysis when it went out into the world. All that is part of the tradition which we have inherited, and from which, if we are to do our job, we cannot escape.

I turn, I hope in that spirit, to my particular topic.

One must begin with a distinction which has been fully understood only in quite recent years. Suppose we start by saying (as many would say) that the capital of an economy is its stock of real goods, with power of producing further goods (or utilities) in the future—the stock of such goods existing in the economy at a moment in time. That, in strictness, is no more than a list—what in English, but not in American, we would call an inventory. How do we aggregate it, as for macroeconomic purposes we have to do? We cannot aggregate except by adding money values; how do we deflate that money aggregate, so as to get a measure of Real Capital? There are, in principle, two main ways.

The first, which on the analogy of other aggregates, such as consumption, may seem the more natural, is to deflate by an index of the prices of the capital goods themselves. (It may not be easy to find a suitable index, but that is not here my concern.) It is, theoretically, a possible measure; to distinguish it from the other, to which I shall be coming, I call it Volume of Capital. It has the property, it will be noticed, that as between two economies which have capital stocks that are physically identical, Volume of Capital must be the same.

It may well be objected, and has often been objected, that Volume of Capital misses the essential fact about capital—that the utilities of capital goods are indirect. The values of capital goods are derived values, capitalized values of future net products. If these future products are valued at current prices of products, the resultant capitalised values should be better indicators of the true values of the capital goods than their actual market values, which are influenced by expectations of changing values of products. These 'corrected' capital values could be aggregated; but since they have been built up from product prices, not capital good prices, they can only be deflated by an index of product prices, if they are to be used as a measure of Real Capital. Real Capital, in this sense, does not have the invariance property; it may be changed, without any change in the physical goods, by the mere admission of new information. I call this other measure Value of Capital.

When the distinction is expressed in this statistical (or quasi-statistical) manner, it would seem that we need have no difficulty in living with it. We can keep both in play, using one for some purposes, the other for others. We may nevertheless have some difficulty in explaining ourselves. Both, as described, are measures of Real Capital; but what is Real Capital? We cannot say that the two measures are two measures of the same thing—as one may say that one buys a pound of something, or a dollar's worth of it, when the price of the thing is a dollar a pound. The Real Capital that is being measured is different.

If it is capital in the volume sense that is being measured, capital is physical goods; but in the value sense capital is not physical goods. It is a sum of values which may conveniently be described as a Fund. A Fund that may be embodied in physical goods in different ways. There are these two senses of Real Capital which need to be distinguished.

I do of course borrow the term Fund from the history, and to the history I now turn. I am going to maintain that the distinction is quite ancient; it divides economists, ancient and modern, into two camps. There are some for whom Real Capital is a Fund—I shall call them Fundists; and there are some for whom it consists of physical goods. It is tempting to call the latter Realists;[1] but since one wants to emphasize that both concepts are *real*, this is not satisfactory. I shall venture in this paper to call them Materialists. (Materialists, I mean in the sense of Dr. Johnson's refutation of Berkeley's idealism—'striking his foot with mighty force against a large stone, till he rebounded from it, *I refute it thus*'. There will be some at least of my Materialists who are worthy followers of Dr. Johnson.)

One of these was Edwin Cannan, the teacher of Lionel Robbins and the founder of the economics school of the London School of Economics and Political Science. A beautiful

[1] As I have done myself in a short passage in my *Capital and Time* (Oxford, 1973), p.13. I have since become convinced that Materialist is better.

illustration of the opposition with which I am here concerned is to be found in Cannan's comments on capital in Adam Smith.[2] Cannan was convinced that Smith was in a muddle. I do not think that he was in a muddle; he was simply a throughgoing Fundist, and to the Materialist Cannan the Fundist position was quite incomprehensible. Cannan: 'The capital [in Smith] is often spoken of as if it were something other than the goods themselves.' That is just the point.

Not only Adam Smith, but all (or nearly all) of the British Classical Economists were Fundists; so was Marx (how else should he have invented 'Capitalism'?); so was Jevons. It was after 1870 that there was a Materialist Revolution. It is not the same as the Marginalist Revolution; for some of the Marginalists, such as Jevons and Böhm–Bawerk, kept the Fundist flag flying. But most economists, in England and in America, went Materialist.[3] Materialism, indeed, is characteristic of what is nowadays reckoned to be the 'neo-classical' position. Not only Cannan, but Marshall and Pigou, and J. B. Clark, were clearly Materialists. Anyone, indeed, who uses a Production Function, in which Product is shown as a function of labour, capital, and technology, supposed separable, confesses himself to be (at least while he is using it) a Materialist.

What about Keynes? Keynes, of course, was brought up as a Materialist, and there are no more than slight signs, in the *General Theory*, that he had departed from the Materialist position. So it is perfectly possible to be a Keynesian and yet to be a Materialist. But the rethinking of capital theory and of growth theory, which followed from Keynes, and from Harrod on Keynes, led to a revival of Fundism. If the Production Function is a hallmark of Materialism, the capital–output ratio is a hallmark of modern Fundism. That, in the briefest of outline, is the story; how it happened I shall now attempt

[2] Cannan, *A Review of Economic Theory* (London, 1929), pp. 145–50.
[3] But there was at least one important American Fundist, F. W. Taussig. Irving Fisher is harder to place, since he, at least sometimes, could see both sides. But it is interesting to find that Cannan thought Fisher, like himself, to be a Materialist.

to explain.

Let us go back to the Classics. Why were the Classical Economists Fundists? It is not easy to see, just from looking at their works; they take their Fundism so much for granted that they do not need to justify it. Surely the reason is that it came to them from outside—from business practice, from accounting practice.

Even to this day, accountants are Fundists. It is not true, accountants will insist, that the plant and machinery of a firm are *capital*; they are not capital, they are assets. Capital, to the accountant, appears on the liabilities side of the balance-sheet; plant and machinery appear on the assets side. Capital, accordingly, is a Fund that is embodied in the assets.

The origin of accounting is in the business of the merchant; accounting categories, to this day, bear the mark of their mercantile origin. It was the merchant who was the original Fundist. It is the merchant who thinks of his capital as a Fund that is invested in a stock of sealeable goods. It is in the Fund sense that capital 'circulates'; the physical goods do not circulate, but the Fund does. It is the Fund that is 'turned over'. The stock of goods in the merchant's possession is one thing (the most he will admit is that it is the form that is taken by his capital at the moment); his capital, he will surely say, is something more permanent.

These were the business terms which came naturally to the Classical Economists. They had no reason to depart unnecessarily from the businessman's language. This was the system of thought that the businessmen of their time were using; they just followed it. It is true that they were thinking of the whole (national) economy, not of the single business; but this, they surely felt, made no difference. It did not need to make much difference. They could think (as Henry Thornton, in particular, most surely did think) of the whole economy as having a balance-sheet, constructed by consolidation of the balance-sheets of the single businesses; in the consolidation, the liabilities of one unit would be cancelled against the assets of another, but no item would be transferred from the liabilities to the assets side. So, even when all debts and paper claims had been cancelled, there would remain on the assets side the real goods (and balance of external claims), on the liabilities side the Capital—still a Fund. It need not be thought of as a debt owed by the nation to itself; it is the same kind of thing as the Capital of the single business.

The way would thus be open for Classical Fundism if the whole economy consisted of merchants; how far, however, could it cope with businesses of other kinds? It was necessary, from the start, to deal with businesses of other kinds; but for the first of the extensions that were needed, Fundism did not do at all badly. It is often thought that the notion of capital as 'advances to labourers' took its origin from observation of agriculture, so it is labelled physiocratic; and it is true that if one looks only at the economic literature it is with the French physiocrats that it seems to come in. But so far at least as the British Classical Economists are concerned, it is more convincingly interpreted as a fitting of agricultural experience into the mercantile pattern. The farmer, like the merchant, 'turns over' his capital, buying the services of labour, as the merchant buys his stock in trade; selling the product of that labour when it is ready to be marketed. So the Fundist concept of capital could be carried over to agriculture, surviving the transition. It seemed, on the whole, quite a good fit.

The farmer, of course, used land as well as capital, but that land was a separate factor of production no one doubted. The rent of the land must be deducted from the 'gross' profit on any agricultural operation before the 'net' profit was arrived at; it would be the rate of net profit on the Capital Fund that competition would tend to equalize.

Classical economics was three-factor economics, and we can now see that the triad had deeper roots than is commonly supposed. Labour is a flow, land is a stock (as stock and flow are used in modern economics); but capital is neither stock nor flow—it is a Fund. Each of the three factors has its own attribute, applicable to itself but to neither of the others.

Labour works *on* land *through* capital, not on capital nor with capital. The place of each of the factors in the productive process is sharply distinguished.

The Classical Economists, so interpreted, are rather consistent; among their successors, in the latter part of the century, consistency disappears. Not all of those who went Marginalist went Materialist, and those who did go Materialist did so in different ways. The case of Walras, for instance, is quite peculiar. I feel fairly sure that he is to be reckoned as a Materialist; but the reason for his Materialism is his interest in particular capital goods, appearing (of course) in his work as a part of his general determination to work with an *n*-goods model. Yet his Materialism may antedate that determination, and may have been one of the things which impelled him towards it. He says that he took his view of capital from his father, and Auguste Walras (writing in 1849) would certainly seem to have been a Materialist, even an extreme Materialist. 'Capitals' (*capitaux*) to him are capital goods; 'incomes' (*revenus*) are income goods; they are distinguished by multiple (*successive*) uses against single uses and by that alone. Carriages, carts, steam-engines are *capitals*; a glass of wine, a round of beef, a candle are *incomes*. *'Le revenu, ainsi que son nom l'indique, c'est ce qui revient; or, ce qui revient, c'est ce qui s'en va.'*[4]

One must yet beware, in father and son alike, of mistaking for a theoretical approach what is no more than a peculiarity of the French language, the restrictiveness, the deliberate restrictiveness, of its vocabulary. It may well be that much French Materialism is only apparent, a matter of linguistics rather than economics.

The case of Marshall is here more interesting. Marshall's Materialism is much more clearly to be explained by events—by the now achieved Industrial Revolution—the rise in importance of plant and machinery. The Classical schema, as we have seen, began with trade and was extended to agriculture;

---

[4] *Théorie de la richesse sociale* (Paris, 1849), pp. 53–4.

so long as stocks and work in progress were the main part of the manufacturer's physical assets it could be extended, in much the same way, to manufacture also. But when a large part of his capital became *fixed* in plant and machinery, a candidate had appeared for factor status, which did not fit into the classical triad. What was to be done?

Before considering what happened in the economics, it will be useful to turn again to the accounting aspect. The rise of the Machine had already presented the accountant with a parallel problem. What did the accountant do about it?

So long as he had nothing to consider but mercantile transactions, his task in principle was simple. For it is characteristic of the business of the merchant that it is divisible into separate units. Every bale of cotton or pound of cheese which ever forms part of his stock is acquired at a particular date and sold at a particular date; purchase, retention, and sale constitute a separable transaction. (Complete separation is of course not attained in practice, since there are overheads which have to be allocated; but it is so nearly attained that it sets the pattern.) So the accounts of the merchant may be regarded as a bundle of separate accounts. Purchases and sales are indeed going on continually, so that if they are set out in a time sequence, the separate accounts will overlap; it is only if an account were prepared for the whole history of the business, from first setting-up to final closing-down, that a record of purchases and sales would tell the whole story. In any arbitrary, say annual, period there must be transactions which have started before the beginning of the period, but are completed within the period; there must similarly be transactions which are begun within the period but not completed when it is ended. These, however, in the case of a mercantile business cause the minimum of trouble. They can be dealt with by the accepted rule of never taking a profit on any transaction before it is completed. The initial stock of the year will then be brought in *at cost*; and the final stock will be valued at cost in the same manner.[5]

But what was to be done, on these principles, with plant and machinery? The use of land, being regarded as a permanency, could be brought in as a regular charge; but the plant and machinery is not expected to last indefinitely, though its use is spread over a time which is longer than the accounting period. It is important to observe that it is the extension of the use to a duration which is longer than the accounting period which creates the difficulty. There would be no difficulty, here as in the mercantile case, if the account were drawn up for the whole life of the business, from first setting-up to final closing-down.[6] It is for the annual account that there is the problem. The cost of the machine has to be set against a series of sales, the sales of the outputs to which it contributes, but some of these sales are sales of the present year, some are later and some, maybe, earlier. There is thus a problem of imputation; how much is to be reckoned into the costs of this year, and how much into the costs of other years? It is just the same problem as the allocation of overheads, and to that, as is now well known, there is no firm *economic* solution.

Neither has the accountant found a solution—only a name and a set of (essentially arbitrary) rules. The 'depreciation quotas' must add to unity, but that is all that is known, at all firmly, about them. The form of the account is preserved, but only by bringing in, as the capital which is supposed to be invested in the machine at the beginning of the year, that part which has not been absorbed (by being allocated as a cost to the output of preceding years) and by reckoning as the capital invested at the end of the year that part which has not been absorbed in those years nor in this year—so that it is left to be

[5] There is of course the qualification that an expected *loss* may be taken in advance: 'cost or market value whichever is the lower'. But this does not affect the principle.

[6] It was the realization that the economist, unlike the accountant, need not be bound down by annuality, unless he chooses, which was one of the things that prompted me to write *Capital and Time*.

carried forward to the future. This is in fact what accountants did (probably what they had to do) as soon as they were confronted with the problem. It is what they still do, even to this day.

We have had plenty of opportunity in the present century to understand how arbitrary the accountant's depreciation quotas are. We have seen them battered by inflation, and we have seen them manipulated by tax authorities in the interests of fiscal policy. Late nineteenth-century economists had much less of this experience, so it is not surprising to find that they began by taking the accountant's depreciation quotas much too seriously. That is true of both schools. It is true of the surviving Fundists (such as the Austrians) who conceived of investment in a fixed capital as equivalent to a bundle of investments in circulating capital. If one-tenth of the cost of a machine of ten-year life could be imputed as cost to the product of each year, the machine was equivalent to ten investments in circulating capital, one with an investment period of one year, one of two years . . . and one of ten years. It was the accountant's depreciation quotas which did the trick.

It is also true of Marshall. He also relied upon the accountant's 'solution', but in a different way. It was an essential element in his concept of long-period equilibrium. In the short period, Marshall tells us, when 'the producers have to adjust their supply to the demand as best they can with the appliances at their disposal', the 'income' derived from those 'appliances' is a *quasi-rent*.[7] It is called a quasi-rent by analogy with the rent of land; in all of his short-period theory Marshall has Ricardo's rent theory very much in mind. Now the rent which is determined as a surplus, in Ricardo's manner, makes no allowance for depreciation; in Ricardo, land being 'indestructable', no such allowance is of course required. Marshall, however, does think of a deduction being made,

---

[7] A. Marshall, *Principles*, 8th edn. (London, 1922), p. 376.

even in the short period, though Ricardo has given him no help in determining what that deduction should be. It is true that Marshall is so reticent on the matter that he can easily be misunderstood; one has to read him quite carefully to discover whether quasi-rents are to be taken gross or net. He does, however, say in a definitional chapter of *Principles*:

We cannot properly speak of the interest yielded by a machine. If we use the term *interest* at all, it must be in relation not to the machine itself but to its money value. For instance if the work done by a machine which cost £100 is worth £4 a year net, that machine is yielding a quasi-rent of £4 which is equivalent to interest at four per cent, on its original cost; but if the machine is worth only £80 now, it is yielding five per cent on its present value. [pp. 74–5].

This seems conclusive.

It is indeed quite remarkable how little there is in Marshall's book about depreciation. There is a footnote in which he recognizes that it is a problem, but the footnote just ends with a reference to an accounting textbook.[8] He has evidently decided that for his purposes, the accountant's solution will do. Gross can in that way be reduced to net, and it is net returns that are equalized by competition in the long period.

That is what Marshall says, but in the forty years which followed on the publication of his *Principles*, the strangest things must have happened to teaching on this point, even among his closest followers. One had heard rumours that there was a good deal of confusion between 'gross' and 'net' among Cambridge teachers, and a strong piece of evidence in support of them has now come to hand. In his chapter on the marginal efficiency of capital in the *General Theory*, Keynes is careful not to call his Q's quasi-rents, and rightly so, since they are gross of depreciation, so they are *not* what Marshall meant by *quasi-rent*. But why are they symbolized by Q? It

8 *Principles*, pp. 354–5.

has naturally been assumed that Q stands for quasi-rents in many post-Keynesian writings. We now know that in an earlier draft the Q's *were* called quasi-rents.[9] Keynes made a correction, or semi-correction, in the final version, but the confusion is betrayed.

The fact is that until the new wind began to blow, in the mid-twenties, very little interest had been taken in Cambridge in capital theory. Take the case of Pigou. One of the remarkable changes introduced into the later editions of *The Economics of Welfare* is a chapter entitled 'Maintaining Capital Intact'. There was no such chapter in the first or second edition. It makes its appearance in the third (1928), by which time the problem of defining saving, in conditions of changing prices, had been brought to light in the work of Robertson.[10] In the fourth edition (1932) it is considerably altered; and there is a further version, in an important article (1935) which looks as if it was intended as the basis of another revision.[11] Pigou, it is clear, was very bothered; and one can see why.

It was only a part of the problem of capital with which he thought himself to be concerned; he was trying to look at that one part in isolation. In spite of its 'Welfare' colouring, the subject of his book was the Social Product (or 'dividend' as he calls it): how it is measured, what makes it large or small, how it is distributed. The Social Product of one particular period ('year') is considered, almost, in isolation. Having chosen that way of posing his problem, he is led (almost inevitably) to what would nowadays be called a 'Production Function' approach. Even so, he might have found himself confronting the general problem of measuring capital—for

---

[9] Keynes, *Collected Writings* (London and New York, 1971-), Vol. XIII, pp. 425–6.
[10] D. H. Robertson, *Banking Policy and the Price Level* (London, 1926).
[11] A. C. Pigou, 'Net Income and Capital Depletion', *Economic Journal* (June 1935), 178.

how can we make a static comparison, between two economies whose capital stocks are different, without having some means of comparing their capital stocks? Pigou did not, at first, raise this wide question, though Robertson, at much the same date, could already see that it was involved.[12] He confined himself to what arose in the measurement of income, in the single year—the measurement of the investment component, the reduction of gross investment to net. (This, of course, already implies a problem of capital measurement—the comparison of the beginning-year and the end-year capital stocks.)

Pigou's approach is strictly Materialist. He does indeed recognize that the business concept of capital is different, but

for economics the stock of capital existing at any time is a collection of objects, the extent of which is a purely physical fact. . . . the size of the stock is not . . . *affected* by its value; it is exactly the same . . . whether that value is large or small. [*Economic Journal* 1935, p. 235.]

He goes on to draw from this the important conclusion, echoes of which are to be found in many more recent writings:

A distinction should be drawn between changes which, while leaving the element still as productive as ever, bring nearer the day of sudden and final break-down, and physical changes which reduce its current productivity and so rentable value. With the former sort of change, until the breakdown occurs, the capital stock is, I suggest, best regarded as intact, just as it is best regarded as intact despite the nearer approach of a day that will make a part of it obsolete. [Ibid., p. 238.]

I shall not discuss Pigou's treatment in detail; enough has been said to indicate its Materialist character. For the purpose which Pigou had in mind, it may well be defensible (as I shall show), but it can hardly be regarded as general; so it is not

[12] See Robertson's paper 'Wage Grumbles', reprinted in his *Economic Fragments* (London, 1931). I have a particular affection for that paper since it was through it that I myself first came into touch with its author.

surprising that there were quarters where it was not well received. I think not so much of the 'user cost' chapter in Keynes's *General Theory*, which I regard as an unsuccessful (and for Keynes's purpose unnecessary) attempt to bridge the gap. The most direct statement of an opposing view came from Professor Hayek.

Hayek's first paper on the subject was already in preparation when Pigou's article appeared in 1935.[13] He further developed it in his *Pure Theory of Capital* (1941) and in a paper in *Economica* which is a reply to a further note by Pigou.[14] Hayek, of course, was a Fundist, but a very sophisticated Fundist, deeply preoccupied with the problems of ignorance and uncertainty which come to the fore as soon as one thinks of capital value as being determined by expectations of the future. It was the omission of this aspect which set him against the Materialism of Pigou. His striking illustration— of the machinery installed to produce a fashion good, required within the year but not afterwards, so that at the end of the year the machine which is physically intact has lost its value— is directed to show the economic irrelevance of physical identity. *In general*, so it seems to me, Hayek is right.[15]

I shall not attempt to carry the story further, except to suggest that we may get a useful light upon more recent differences if we look at them in terms of this interesting controversy between Pigou and Hayek. Pigou, I think one can now see, was working within a model—a rather restrictive model but a useful model, a model which for certain purposes we would most of us still wish to employ. Its central concept was the Social Product, a *measurable* Social Product. It has

[13] F. Hayek, 'The Maintenance of Capital', *Economica* 2, (Aug. 1935), 241–74.
[14] See Hayek, 'Maintaining Capital Intact', *Economica*, 8 (Aug. 1941), 276–80, and Pigou, 'Maintaining Capital Intact', ibid. 271–5.
[15] In my own contribution to the same discussion I came down mainly on Hayek's side. The positive part of my paper is reprinted in *Capital and Time*, pp. 164–6.

now become clear that one cannot measure a Social Product of the Welfare type with which Pigou was concerned unless one assumes that wants are unchanging—or that some kind of Social Welfare Function is unchanging—and that cuts out the sort of variation over time which is the root of Hayek's example. In Pigou's world the Hayek problem could not arise. In general, of course, it does arise. There are bound to be odd cases which will not fit into the Pigou model.

I do not mean to imply that attention to odd cases is the principal reason for the revival of Classical Fundism. It is one of the reasons; there are plenty of economists who make their living by trading in odd cases, which make splendid subjects for little notes in journals. There are other reasons which are more substantial. Fundism, as I have emphasized, is the businessman's concept of capital; social accounting, which has brought economists into closer relation with business accounting, was bound to induce a revival of Fundism. So was attention to planning. Planning is forward-looking, and the Fundist concept of capital is forward-looking; they fit in. For such and such a development, how much capital will be required? It is capital in the Fund sense to which such questions are relevant.

When Fundism is looked at in this light, we can see that there may be a place for Materialism also. If Fundism is forward-looking, Materialism is backward-looking, for it is concerned with the capital goods existing at the moment, goods which have been brought into being in the past. 'Bygones are bygones', but there are still some purposes for which we have to go to the past. Our statistics, in particular, always relate to the past. One cannot measure capital, statistically, excepting in terms of its history, valuing, of course, not at historical cost, but at doctored historical cost, or replacement cost. There is a striking example of this in the book by J.R.S. Revell, *The Wealth of the Nation* (1967), an inquiry conducted in Cambridge, England, a place that must often appear as a headquarters of the New Fundism. Revell's calculation of the National Capital of Britain would have appealed to Pigou;[16] he had to be Materialist, because as a statistician he could be nothing else.[17] There is nothing else that can be used in macroeconometrics; so it is macroeconometrics itself which is on trial—but that, perhaps, is as it should be.

[16] I am aware that in his last note on the subject, Pigou (*Economica*, 1941) dissociated himself from the replacement cost measure of capital, pointing to the case where the article to be replaced 'had become impossible to produce' as a reason for rejecting it. I do not think he was well advised to make this concession. He would have done better to insist that it was one of the 'odd cases' that he was leaving out.

[17] For further discussion of this matter of measurement, see my *Capital and Time*, ch. XIII and *Social Framework*, 4th edn. 1971), Appendix D.

VIII   THE DISASTER POINT IN RISK THEORY

1. In the paper on Portfolio Selection, which is printed in my *Critical Essays in Monetary Theory* (1967, pp. 103-25), I followed what has become the conventional approach, supposing that the 'prospect' of each available investment could be expressed in terms of the first two moments of a probability distribution (e, s). I did this, in spite of a feeling that many of the 'prospects' involved in actual business decisions are by no means normally distributed, but are highly skewed; and that when we speak of *risk*, it is the skewness of the distribution, not its variance, that we principally have in mind. I therefore extended my dicussion, to a limited extent, to take account of skewness; but I made no pretence that the extension was satisfactory.

There is, however, a passage, in that same paper, in which I made some examination of the alternative 'Bernouillian' approach to risk-bearing; an approach which has the obvious merit that it imposes no restriction upon the 'shape' of the prospect, as does the (e, s) approach, at least in effect. I nevertheless rejected that approach, not on account of its adherence to 'cardinal utility' (for I accepted the demonstration, by Samuelson and others,[1] that in this field of choice under uncertainty, the use of a cardinal function is permissible) but for another reason. In the particular case of a linear marginal utility function, the only case where it is easy to build a bridge between the (e, s) theory and the Bernouillian theory, so that either approach is applicable, we get absurd results.[2] Nevertheless, since writing, and largely as a result of thinking over the work on this subject of Professor Arrow[3] (with whom, it will

---

[1] *Econometrica*, 1951.

[2] *Critical Essays*, pp. 114-17.

[3] K. J. Arrow, *Aspects of the theory of risk-bearing* (Helsinki, 1965). The initial impetus, which led me to this reconsideration, came, however,

be seen, I am not in complete agreement), I have come to feel that I should give the Bernouillian approach some further consideration.

2. I begin by setting out the problem in the same terms as before. An investor, with capital K, has to choose among n securities. x_j is the amount invested in the jth security, so that $\Sigma x_j = K$ $(j = 1, \ldots n)$. There are m eventualities, or 'states of the world'. The outcome of one unit of capital, invested in the jth security, is known for each eventuality; for the ith eventuality, it is a_{ij}. Thus the outcome of the whole port-folio, in the ith eventuality, is $\Sigma a_{ij}x_j$ over all j. We call this v_i.

We are now to make the Bernouillian assumption, that the investor acts in such a way as to maximize $U = \Sigma p_i u (v_i)$, where the sum is taken over all eventualities, where the p are *given* probabilities, and where $u (v_i)$ is the *total* utility of the outcome v_i. There is, however, a question, as Arrow has shown, of what utility functions are in such a construc-tion admissible.

It would be very convenient if we could find a utility function which was such that it gave a distribution which was independent of scale; that is to say, when p's and a's are unchanged, the chosen (x_j) would be such that (x_j/K) was independent of K. If such a function could be found, it would serve as a standard of reference, a most convenient standard of reference. It is Arrow's contention that there is no such function which is admissible; but here, as I shall explain, I disagree.

3. Let us see what properties such a function would have to have. The investor will be in equilibrium at a particular (x_j) if the marginal utilities $(\partial U/\partial x_j)$ are there equal. If when the (x_j) are changed in equal proportions, the equilibrium conditions are still satisfied, these marginal utilities must remain equal, that is to say, they must all be changed in the

from correspondence with Prof. S.C. Tsiang, to whom, and also to Prof. J.L. Ford, of Sheffield, I should like to make acknowledgements.

same proportion. Now since the v_i's are linear functions of the x_j's, an equi-proportional change in the x_j's implies an equi-proportional change in the v_i's. So we can work in terms of v's, noting that (by the Bernouillian assumption) the marginal utility of each v is a function of that v only. In fact $(\partial U/\partial v_i) = p_i u'(v_i)$.

It follows[4] that the $(\partial U/\partial x_j)$ will remain equal when the x_j change in the same proportion, if the elasticities of the $u'(v_i)$ are the same for all v_i. But $u'(v)$ is the same for all v_i. But $u'(v)$ is the *same* curve for each v_i, the different $u'(v_i)$ being simply expressions of different points along that same curve. Thus the condition requires, in general, that the elasticity of $u'(v)$ should be constant. Thus

$$u'(v) = A(1-\alpha)v^{-\alpha}$$

as it will be convenient to write it, and

$$u(v) = B + A v^{1-\alpha}$$

by integration.

A, B, α are all constants. If $u'(v)$ is to be positive for positive α, $A(1-\alpha)$ must be positive. And if (as Bernouilli and his followers assume) $u'(v)$ diminishes with v, α must be positive.

We still have to distinguish the cases in which α is $>$ or < 1. (The case in which $\alpha = 1$, so that, as appears from integrating v^{-1}, total utility takes a logarithmic form, though it was the case that was specially considered by Bernouilli, needs for our purpose no particular attention.) If $\alpha < 1$, A must be positive; B can have either sign. But here, if $v = 0$, $u = B$; while as v increases, u increases indefinitely. If $\alpha > 1$, A must be negative, and B must be taken to be positive (as Ramsey[5] long ago observed). Here, as v increases, u tends to B asymptotically; but as v tends to zero, u diminishes indefinitely.

In no case, it will be noticed, does the construction make sense for negative v. When $\alpha > 1$, and v is negative, either u is imaginary, or alternatively $u(-v) = u(v)$, *so that u increases*

[4] See Explanatory note on p. 167.

[5] F. Ramsey, 'Mathematical Theory of Saving' (*Economic Journal*, 1928).

as v becomes more negative, which is surely absurd. It seems fair to conclude that negative v must be excluded.

This could, on occasion, be troublesome; but in the particular application, to Portfolio Selection theory, it does not necessarily matter. All it means is that we must interpret the outcome of an investment to mean the gross outcome, including 'repayment of capital', not the net outcome, or yield. For on that interpretation, if the field of investment is what is nowadays the normal type (including cash, bonds, and equities carrying limited liability) the worst that can happen is total loss. (I shall have a word to say later about other applications.) If that is granted, all a_{ij} can be taken to be non-negative. And if all x_j are non-negative, all v_i must be non-negative. We need not attend to negative v's.

I now come to the point that has been made by Professor Arrow.[6] He observes that if there is a single security which offers a chance of a very large gain—much larger than is offered by any other—then, if the utility function is unbounded upwards, an investor who acts on Bernouillian principles will put his whole fortune into that single investment. He will do this if the gain that is offered is large enough, even though the chance of getting it is exceedingly small. But this is just the 'Petersburg Paradox' behaviour which Bernouilli was trying to exclude! On this ground we must rule out a utility function which is unbounded upwards—in particular, the function just constructed with $\alpha > 1$. (It also means that we must exclude the logarithmic function, Bernouilli's own, since that also is unbounded upwards.) With this I agree.

The same, however, does not seem to apply (as he apparently supposes) to the function with $\alpha > 1$, the Ramsey function which economists I think would on other grounds prefer. What does it matter if the utility function is unbounded downwards? All that is implied, if the utility function is of the type described, with $\alpha > 1$, is that the investor will never

[6] Arrow, op. cit., p. 26.

put the *whole* of his capital into an investment where there is a finite possibility of total loss. He may put some of his capital into such an investment; but so long as the rest is put into investments where there is no such possibility, he is not undertaking a finite possibility of total loss, over his whole portfolio. We all know about the gambler who stakes his last shirt on a wager, but if we are looking for a standard case of investment behaviour, it need not incommode us if such extreme cases of gambling are excluded from it. There is nothing to stop the investor, whose behaviour is included, having 'a bit of a flutter' with a *part* of his capital.

4. So far, then, there seems to be no reason why we should not agree to take the case that we have been defining as a standard case. I do not mean by this that all problems of portfolio selection should be forced into this pattern—quite the contrary. What I mean is that we are free to use it as a standard of reference. What it gives us is a simple case, which is such that the behaviour which it implies is relatively easy to establish; by comparison with it we can extend our view to other possible kinds of behaviour. There are in fact other kinds, not really so difficult to distinguish in practice, where behaviour may be expected to diverge from the standard behaviour in determinable ways.

In the standard case the proportional distribution of the portfolio is independent of its size. This requires, we have found, that the marginal utility $u'(v)$ should have constant elasticity (elasticity < 1 and so $\alpha > 1$). Constant elasticity is not easy to test directly; but the behaviour at the extremes, which it implies, is easier to deal with. (It should be emphasized that in risk theory, much more than in consumer theory, extremes are relevant. The changes in consumption which follow from most price-changes are fairly small; we can therefore confine attention to a small region of the general utility function, and over that small region we may substitute any simple function which fits reasonably well. Here, however, in risk theory, the *possibility* of major disaster is one of the things that must always be taken into account. We cannot avoid the extremes.

Take first the upper extreme, where v is large. At this end I would claim that we shall not often want to introduce a significant departure from the standard function. In the standard case, as v increases indefinitely, marginal utility continues to diminish, but always remains positive. Is not this what we should expect? If there were two securities which offered the same outcome in all eventualities but one, but in that particular eventuality one offered more than the other, the rational investor would surely choose the one which offered the better prospect, however good the prospects were. He would always go for that which offered a million plus one, rather than that which offered no more than a million. But so small a difference, between two large numbers, would never outweigh a perceptible increase in risk on the other side. This is precisely what the 'constant elasticity' curve shows.

It is certainly true that we get a different result if (by analogy with consumer theory—but, as just explained, I think it is a false analogy) we allow ourselves to work with a linear form of marginal utility curve. For if the marginal utility curve is linear (and the same will happen, indeed, with any polynomial) a sufficient increase in v must cause $u'(v)$ to become negative. There must, that is, be a point of satiation. And a further increase in wealth, beyond the satiation point, must be a nuisance!

That an increase in the supply of some particular commodity, beyond a satiation point, should be a nuisance is easy to admit. It is not so easy to accept it for wealth in general, when (*ex hypothesi*) that wealth can be held in a variety of forms. A milder form of satiation, with marginal utility falling to zero, at the satiation point, but not falling further, makes better sense. As I have indicated, I do not think that even this can reasonably be regarded as 'normal' behaviour; it is possible, however, that on occasion we may wish to go that far.

It is not in the least surprising to find that with a utility function that has a satiation point the investor will 'play for safety' as he gets richer. With standard behaviour, as K increases, all x's increase proportionately, and therefore all v's increase proportionally. The constant elasticity keeps the marginal utilities $u'(v_i)$ in the same ratios, to one another, as before. But with the new function a proportional increase in v's will reduce the marginal utilities of the larger v's more rapidly than those of the smaller. When the satiation point is far away this effect will be negligible; but the nearer it is approached, the more important the effect becomes. When that happens, the equilibrium of the portfolio can only be restored by a relative reduction in the amounts that are put into investments with relatively large (favourable) outcomes. The chance of gain which would have balanced a chance of relatively large loss when K was small will fail to balance it when K becomes larger. But it is odd to interpret such behaviour as an increased aversion to risk; since the reason for it is the approach to satiation, it is more natural to reckon it as an indication that the remuneration for risk-bearing has become less attractive. We need not be so ordinalist as to refuse to say that!

5. Much more important, in my opinion, is the possibility of a bias at the other end. It is implied in the standard assumptions, which we have so far been using, that marginal utility becomes infinite when $v = 0$. The zero point is thus a disaster point, which must at all costs be avoided. But why, in general, should the disaster point be at $v = 0$? There are many practical cases, such as that of the small saver who is dependent upon income from his investments, or that of the charitable foundation which has commitments which it feels itself bound to meet, where an outcome much better than zero will yet spell disaster. We can deal with such cases, indeed rather easily, by a simple but most important extension of the construction we have so far been using.

Put marginal utility equal to $(v - c)^{-\alpha}$, so that it becomes infinite at $v = c$. This extended form is as easy to use as the other, and its additional parameter gives it additional flexibility.

Its consequences follow at once. Since $v_i = \Sigma\, a_{ij}\, x_j$, and $K = \Sigma\, x_j$, $v_i - c = \Sigma\, [a_{ij} - (c/K)]\, x_j$. Maximization is therefore exactly the same as with the standard function, save that all unit outcomes are written down by (c/K). If K is large relatively to c, the write-down is negligible; so the optimum portfolio will be much the same as with the standard function. But as K diminishes, relatively to c, the write-down will take effect. Some of the $a_{ij} - (c/K)$ will then be likely to go negative. The investor will thus tend to avoid securities which have these low a_{ij}–securities, that is, which have a very bad outcome in some eventualities. He will avoid such risky securities. He will 'play for safety' as he gets poorer, or as he gets nearer to his disaster point.

It is evident from the case of the charitable foundation (but the point is more generally valid) that the disaster point depends upon circumstances; it is perfectly conceivable that a large capital should carry with it a high disaster point. If, as K rises, c rises proportionately, there is no 'write-down' (or no further write-down); so we return, in effect, to the standard case. The distribution of the portfolio will be independent of K. If we re-define the standard in this manner, we can regard a change in the (c/K) ratio as a principal way in which there may be a divergence from standard behaviour. We can admit that the investor will 'play for safety' as he gets richer if, when K rises, c rises faster—as may happen if the additional wealth carries with it additional commitments, or additional responsibilities, which outweigh it. Only if the additional wealth carries with it no additional commitments can we be reasonably sure that the bias will go the other way; the larger K would increase the willingness to bear risks.

6. One of the advantages of this re-statement is that it frees the theory from some of the limitations of the preceding discussion. As we began by stating the Portfolio Selection problem, possibilities were limited by an external floor; the worst that could happen would be *total* loss. That restriction can now be removed. For the disaster point has now ceased to be external, a characteristic of the market on which the investor operates; it has become a subjective characteristic of the investor himself. This widens the scope of the theory considerably.

We can, for instance, abandon the assumption we have hitherto been making, that all x_j are non-negative. We are no longer obliged to look at the assets side of the Portfolio in isolation. The investor can be allowed to borrow, in order to make his investments; he can be allowed, if he has the opportunity, to trade on 'margins'. All that is necessary is that the net value of the portfolio as a whole, in the worst of the eventualities that are taken into account, should be greater than the disaster level (c). Of course it is not excluded that he may be wrong, that the policy that is adopted may in fact lead to disaster; all we assume is that he does not *plan* for disaster.

In these terms, the two-parameter theory can be applied rather widely; and surely it makes sense. It may indeed be claimed that (c/K) is a better indicator of what we mean by risk-aversion than the exponent α. What α measures is acquisitiveness; the degree of desire for large gains. What is measured by (c/K) is the extent of risk that the investor is prepared to take—his willingness to take a chance of large loss. To exhibit the risky choice as a balance between the hope of gain, on the one hand, and the fear of disaster, on the other, is (at the least) intuitively appealing.

I am nevertheless not claiming that the Bernouillian approach, which has been followed in this Note, is all that we need as a basis for risk theory, or even for that particular department of risk theory which is the portfolio problem. I think I have shown that it is a rather effective way of dealing with changes in the investible fund, when the prospects of the available investments (p's and a's) are taken as given. That is to say, it is good at dealing with 'wealth effects'—effects which on the (e, s) approach are not dealt with at all conclusively. When it comes to the consideration of changes in prospects, its comparative advantage is probably less.

That is not to say that it is altogether incompetent to deal with changes in prospects. One can easily show, algebraically, that an improvement in the expected outcome of some particular investment, in some particular eventuality, will raise the marginal utility of that investment relatively to others, so that the amount which is put into that investment should increase. For since

$$U_j = \Sigma_i p_i u'(v_i) a_{ij}$$

and it is only the ith term in the sum which is affected by a rise in a_{ij}, it is clear that the effect of the rise will be compounded (i) of a direct effect on the explicit a_{ij} (ii) of an indirect effect through $u'(v_i)$. This indirect effect will lower U_j (on our assumption about the form of the utility function); but there is exactly the same indirect effect on the marginal utilities of the other investments, so that for each $k (= j)$ the ratio U_j/U_k must rise. But this does not tell us much.

We can nevertheless make some progress along similar lines with more interesting questions. Take for instance the Domar–Musgrave proposition about the effect of a tax with 'perfect loss-offset'.[7] We may simplify by supposing that there are just two investments available: one (A) with a certain outcome in all eventualities, the other (B) uncertain, with varying outcomes. Initially, before the tax is imposed, there is a particular optimum distribution between A and B. If tax with perfect loss-offset is interpreted[8] as an arrangement whereby the difference between A and B outcomes in each eventuality is reduced in a fixed proportion—a part of the gain from B over A, in favourable circumstances, being taken in tax, and a corresponding part of the deficiency, in unfavourable circumstances, being refunded—the investor is placed in the same position as he would have occupied if there had been no change in tax arrangements, but he had held more of his portfolio in A and less in B. This is shown by his former behaviour not to be an optimum position; to restore optimality he must increase his holding of B. But this is not

---

[7] What was said about this proposition in *Critical Essays* (p. 117 n.) can clearly, in the light of the above, be seen to be wrong. That footnote is hereby withdrawn.

[8] It will be noticed that this is a special interpretation, designed in order to bring out the point as simply as possible. It is assumed that there is no tax on the certain outcome A.

because he has become any more willing to bear risk; it is because a part of the risk from investing in B has been taken off him, being assumed by the taxing authority. It is because, as far as he is concerned, B has been made less risky.

These things can be done; but there remains all that part of portfolio theory which is concerned with spreading of risks. It is there, very naturally, that the (e, s) approach is at home; to deal with that by the Bernouillian approach is much more awkward. The same must doubtless be true for econometric applications. So I think that in the end we need both app-roaches. If we check up our results (or our hypotheses) by looking at them both ways, we are likely to avoid many pitfalls. There seems to be no reason why we should not follow that practice.[9]

[9] The Portfolio Selection theory has been taken in this paper in a completely 'static' form. The choice is supposed to be made once and for all, without consideration of the consequences which may follow from today's decision upon the field of choice which may be avail-able in the future. There are bound to be such consequences unless *either* decisions made now cannot be undone, *or* they can be cost-lessly undone. Save in these two extreme cases, there is much more to be said than can be said by a static theory. (For some discussion of these extensions, see the discussion of Liquidity in the second lecture of my *Crisis in Keynesian Economics*, 1974.)

Even in relation to such extensions, this distinctions which have been made in this paper may nevertheless be a help. For it may be that one fruitful way of considering our 'disaster' point is to regard it as the outcome which is so bad that its realization would prevent the investor from continuing his 'game'.

Explanatory note to p. 168

Write U_j for the marginal utility of x_j. Then, if $U = \Sigma p_i\, u(v_i)$, $U_j = \Sigma_i\, p_i\, u'(v_i)\, a_{ij}$; $U_{jk} = \Sigma_i\, p_i\, u''(v_i)\, a_{ij}a_{ik}$. When each x_k increases by $x_k \mathrm{d}\theta$, $(\mathrm{d}U_j/\mathrm{d}\theta) = \Sigma_k \Sigma_i\, p_i\, u''(v_i)\, a_{ij}a_{ik}x_k = \Sigma_i\, p_i\, u''(v_i)\, a_{ij}\, v_i$. If, when this happens, the U_j maintain equal ratios, we must have $(1/U_j)$ $(\mathrm{d}U_j/\mathrm{d}\theta)$ the same for all j. Thus

$$\Sigma_i\, p_i\, [v_i\, u''(v_i) - \lambda\, u'(v_i)]\, a_{ij} = 0$$

for all j, with λ independent of j. Accordingly, if $n > m$ (more securities than eventualities) each of the bracketed expressions must be zero (iso-elasticity). If $n < m$, iso-elasticity implies homotheticity, but not vice versa.

IX EXPLANATIONS AND REVISIONS

Those authors who issue their books in many editions have a regular opportunity of replying to critics; they can show, in the alterations and additions which they make, which of the criticisms that have been made they accept, and which reject. With one major exception,[1] I have not myself followed that practice. I have nevertheless occasionally made what are in effect such replies; some have not been published, while others have appeared in rather miscellaneous places, so they could easily be overlooked. It may perhaps be found to be a convenience if I bring them together.

(i) The Accelerator theory[2]

There is a large part of my *Contribution to the Theory of the Trade Cycle* (1950) which is concerned with the Accelerator model. I did not, of course, invent that model. It was originally introduced, in its Keynesian form (which I used) by Samuelson (1938); its later development owes much to Harrod and to Kaldor. All I did was to elaborate it; I am now not at all sure that the further elaboration was worth while.

The Accelerator model, as such, is wholly non-monetary. It pays little attention, even, to prices. It proceeds, almost entirely, in real terms. And it assumes that its real magnitudes

---

[1] My *Theory of Wages* (1932) when it at last appeared in a second edition (1963) was accompanied by a rather elaborate 'commentary'. But in that case there was so much to withdraw!

The Social Framework is a textbook, which uses facts to illustrate its principles; it has had to appear in new editions, to bring its facts up to date. The alterations which were made in the second edition of *Value and Capital* (1946) were not considerable.

[2] This is an extract from a lecture, entitled 'Real and Monetary Factors in Economic Fluctuations', which was published in the *Scottish Journal of Political Economy* (Nov. 1974).

can be aggregated, so that it can proceed, in the conventional macroeconomic manner, in terms of Output and Employment, Saving and Investment.

In its simplest form, the Accelerator model is very violent; too violent, indeed, to make sense. If saving is geared to output, but investment (net investment) to rate of change of output, saving equals investment gives $sY = cgY$; so $s = cg$ (the Harrod equation) is a condition of equilibrium. But it is an equilibrium that is inherently unstable. Any 'chance' increase in output, raising the rate of growth of output, will induce more investment (the Accelerator) but that will have a Multiplier effect which will raise output further. Output, however, cannot at any time be indefinitely extensible. Thus if the initial equilibrium position was one of less than (Keynesian) Full Employment, any (expansionary) disturbance would drive the economy up to its Full Employment 'ceiling'; but on the ceiling output would have to increase less rapidly than on the way to the ceiling. This would put the Accelerator into reverse; and there is nothing in the simple model which would stop the downward fluctuation, short of complete collapse.

Not even in 1932 (after monetary disaster, of which the Accelerator theory takes no account) was there complete collapse; somehow, to some extent, a bottom, or 'floor' was found. Thus if the Accelerator model was to fit the facts (any facts) it required to be modified, or 'cooled'. In my own version I introduced two 'coolants'; others, however, have been suggested, and I would not now give particular preference to those which I included in my book.

The first of my 'coolants' was the introduction of lags. It is instantaneous adjustment which is so explosive; but it is hard to believe that effects on consumption and investment do not take time to operate. I was able to show that lagged repercussions would not merely lengthen the time that would be taken by the whole process, but would probably dampen the fluctuation considerably. With quite plausible lags, we can readily explain how a boom might peter out without ever reaching a ceiling; and a slump might pass into recovery without ever reaching a floor. This might not happen, but it could happen. The range of phenomena which the model could deal with would thus be considerably widened.

My other 'coolant' was Autonomous Investment. Harrod himself had been reluctant to suppose that all investment activity is closely geared to current output; he allowed for the probable existence of a 'long-range investment' which is relatively independent. I preferred a different description, which was just meant to mark off a part of investment not geared to current output, whether long-range or not. Again with an eye to historical application, I was anxious that the model should not pretend to explain too much. It was easy to show that if one admitted Autonomous Investment that provided a floor.

My Autonomous Investment has been much criticized, but I think that on the whole I would stand by it. I would grant that many things which one might put into the 'autonomous' pigeon-hole would provide no more than a temporary floor; if output continued for very long at the low (slump) level, the support which they gave would fade out. But a temporary floor, if it held for some time, would provide a breathing-space; and in a breathing-space new investment could more confidently be undertaken. In spite of the 'pessimism', properly associated with such a situation, *some* people might surely come round, in the breathing-space, to the view that the depression would not go on for ever.

Two other 'coolants', which I did not use in my book, must now be mentioned. One is 'non-linearity'—the rejection of the Harrodian proportionality between output (or income) and consumption (and therefore saving), which I formally maintained. If, at a low level of output, saving (net saving) disappears, there can clearly be equilibrium with no net investment, so that mere maintenance of capital (gross investment = depreciation) is sufficient to establish a floor. The introduction of such non-linearity is usually associated with distributional considerations, but it need not be so associated. With Friedman's consumption function, consumption depending on *permanent income*, the saving ratio (saving/current income) will be high when income is rising, or abnormally high, low when income is falling or abnormally low. But much the same effect can be represented by lags.

Finally, and perhaps more importantly, there is a qualification which needs to be introduced into the Accelerator itself. Why should investment be geared to rate of change of current output, even with a lag? Only if a rise in output requires an increase in capacity. I was careful, at least at one point in my book, to emphasize the elasticity of capacity; one should think of increased output being produced, in the first place, from existing capacity; only when there was reason to expect that the increased output would go on being required would capacity be increased. But this must mean that on the floor, where there surely is excess capacity, a rise in final demand will not induce a significant amount of investment; only when output has expanded towards a normal level will the Accelerator get to work. It also means that at the 'collision' with the ceiling, arrears of investment, to meet the requirements of that level of output, will still remain to be made up; so it appears to be possible for the economy to remain on its ceiling for longer—indeed far longer—than I supposed. So even a boom which is due to 'explosive' investment—so that it does not peter out—may be less explosive than it appears in my model.

It must, however, be admitted that when the model is modified in these latter ways, it changes its character. It ceases to be a mathematical model, such as might conceivably be used as an econometric hypothesis. Mathematics (or some of it) has provided some illuminating exercises; but it cannot be applied as it stands. The view which I now take about it is the same as that which was taken, in the end, by Dennis Robertson, who, when he looked back at his own early work, concluded:

As to stylised models of the cycle, of the kind now so fashionable, they doubtless have their uses, provided their limitations are clearly understood. We must wait with respectful patience while the econometricians decide whether their elaborate methods are really capable of covering such models with flesh and blood. But I confess that to me at least the forces at work seem so complex, the question whether even the few selected parameters can be relied upon to stay put through the cycle or between cycles so doubtful, that I wonder whether more truth will not in the end be wrung from interpretative studies of the crude data.

(That is from the introduction which he wrote in 1948 to the reprint of his *Study of Industrial Fluctuation*, originally published in 1915.)

(ii) The two kinds of economic history

My *Theory of Economic History* (1969) aroused, as I hoped, some interesting criticisms. There were two review articles, by Professor P.T. Bauer, in *Economica*, and by Professor A. Gerschenkron in the *Economic History Review*. And there were other comments which I received, some subsequently published, some unpublished. I shall make no attempt to reply to them at all fully. In so far as the issues are questions of historical fact, it would be beyond my competence to do so. All I can do is to insist that the facts which I adduced were not meant to be more than illustrative. Thus I am not much disturbed by a demonstration that serfdom in Prussia was less like serfdom in Russia than I had supposed; nor even by the historians' insistence that the dominant interest in the Greek city state was fundamentally agrarian. For my concern was with the emergence of economic patterns; those patterns could be interesting, and important, even when they were not dominant.

I should perhaps have been more aware than I was that there are two kinds of economic history. A large part of the work of economic historians is concerned with one kind, but I was concerned with the other. The part with which I was not concerned deals with standards of living, how they have varied over time, and how those that are attained by one population, or one class of the same population, at the same time, differ from those that are attained by another. Most of

the information that is obtainable on these matters, for all
periods except the most recent, is agricultural; it is the
standard of consumption of agricultural products, chiefly
food products, which is easiest to observe. If one asks why
that standard varies, the answer is chiefly to be found in terms
of population pressure. But it should be noticed that these
have no special relation with human civilization. The standard
of living of an animal population, even of a population of
insects, can be analysed, and is analysed by ecologists, in
corresponding terms. I have no desire to play down these
inquiries; I am sure we need them; but they are not my kind
of economic history.

My concern was with the emergence of economic activities,
in a narrower sense: the emergence of 'economic man', as he
may still be called, economic-calculating man. The 'economic
system' that we now have (in 'socialist' as well as in 'capitalist'
countries) is a system that has been made by him. I wished to
attract attention to the question of how he has come about.

I was well aware that it has been an evolution, a gradual
process. As I said on the first page of my book: 'Economic
history is often presented, and rightly presented, as a process
of specialization; but the specialization is not only a specialization among economic activities, it is also a specialization of
economic activities (what are becoming economic activities)
from activities of other sorts.' That was a principle which I
hoped to keep in mind throughout; but I am now aware that
there were occasions (perhaps there were many occasions)
when I could not prevent it from slipping, or from appearing
to have slipped. For in all those many centuries during which
economic activities were specializing out, what is economic
is always at the same time something else—something else
which, especially to contemporaries, will have seemed to be
of equal, or of greater, importance. The historian, who seeks
to give a rounded view of what happened, will have that very
much in mind. I am sure that he is right to have it in mind. I
do not think that he is doing his business properly when he
interprets the fall of the Roman Empire, or for that matter

the English Civil War, in terms of Marxian concepts which can never have entered the minds of those whose story he is telling. I am aware that my own approach was in danger of falling under the same condemnation. I am convinced that it does not need to do so, but I can now see that I did not safeguard it enough.

The Gerschenkron review was entitled *Mercator Gloriosus*; indeed his main theme was that I had exaggerated the role of the 'merchant'. I think that what I meant by 'merchant' was a little different from his meaning. His merchant is the regular merchant of the economic historian, a person who not only exercises a particular economic function, but is a member of a recognizable social class. My 'merchant' is defined by his economic function only. I was indeed by no means sure that I had given him the right name; there were stages, as I was working out my ideas, when I tried other alternatives. But in the end I could find nothing better than 'merchant'—though it exposed me, as I now see, to misunderstanding, which I should have taken more deliberate steps to ward off.

I insisted, on pages 25–6, that my merchant was a specialized trader; a person who traded, now and then, casually, was not to be regarded as a merchant in my sense. But this should have been backed by a distinction between what might be called 'first degree' traders (who spend most of their time, or most of their working time, trading) and 'second-degree' traders (who do not spend more than a fraction of their time in direct trading, but whose other activities could not exist, in the way they do, except for what they do in their trading time). Farmers, working for the market, and artisans, working for the market, are in this sense second-degree merchants. Their appearance is part of the evolution which I was trying to describe, and to analyse.

Even that, however, is not enough. There is an intervening step, between the casual trader (who just trades, now and then, irregularly) and the second-degree trader, as just defined. One sees it very clearly in the case of farming. The subsistence farmer, who is independent of the market for the greater part of his activity, may nevertheless have, on the side, some cash crop. He is not trading casually, but regularly. So, on my classification, he is a part-time second-degree merchant. Of course it is stretching the term (many will feel that it is stretching it quite intolerably) to regard him as a 'merchant' at all. It is the product of his subsistence farming which re-presents the main part of his standard of living; so, for the historian whose interest is on that side, he is just a subsis-tence farmer, slightly qualified. But from my point of view it is his cash crop that matters. It is by what he does in that way, even if it is no more than a little, that he plays his part in *my* mercantile evolution.

One had to make use of these distinctions, or of something corresponding to them; but it was not easy to keep them in sight all the time. I could have conceded that nearly all of the 'merchants' in Greek city states will have been part-time merchants, perhaps part-time second-degree merchants; but since it was the mercantile evolution (which even so was implied) that was my subject, it was hard not to speak of them as if they were merchants in a fuller sense. We are always doing that sort of thing when we are writing theory; there it is under-stood. I should have been more careful when I was venturing on to a field where it would not be understood so easily.

Most of this could have been put right by the introduction of the distinctions I have just been making, and by some con-sequential improvement in wording; but there is at least one case where the trouble went deeper. I remembered the bride-price when (on p. 65) I was considering the unsuitability of oxen as currency; but I forgot it when I was considering the origin of money itself. I now accept that my account of the origin of money was too *mercantile*. The part played by money in the evolution of the market is essential; but the origin of money must go further back.

(iii) The Ricardo machinery effect

This came up in *A Theory of Economic History* (1969), where it was adduced as a possible reason for the poor 'condition of the people' in the early days of the Industrial Revolution. It was (I hoped) elucidated by the arithmetical example that was given at the end of that book. But one cannot prove anything by a numerical example; and the choice for figures for this was not very satisfactory.[3] I examined the matter further in *Capital and Time* (Chapters VIII and IX); the demonstration that is given there, in terms of its own model, can be claimed to be quite rigorous. But this, I have come to feel, is not all that is required. For the reader of *Capital and Time* has to go a long way, along a rather peculiar path, before he comes to the matter in question. The point is important; it should be possible to state it in a way which would make it more generally accessible.[4]

As the point came up in the *Economic History* book, there were two issues. There is the theoretical question, whether the kind of thing that Ricardo had in mind can happen, and what are the circumstances in which it may happen; and there is the historical question, whether these circumstances are likely to have been realized in the particular case of the Industrial Revolution in England. On the historical issue I do not claim to have made more than a guess, though I am still of the opinion that it is a plausible guess. Doubtless there are many other reasons for the 'lag' in real wages between 1800 and 1850 (I could name several of them myself); all I was suggesting is that what Ricardo had in mind may have been one of the reasons. And it is a particularly interesting reason, since it could well apply in other cases of rapid industrialization, when the industrializing country is not in a position to draw finance from abroad.

---

[3] In the Stationary State, from which my story began in that example, the stability condition which emerged in the later treatment ($a_0 > a_1$ in *Capital and Time* notation) was not satisfied. This does not really affect the argument, but makes it inelegant.

[4] I draw heavily, in what follows, upon a note which I contributed to the *Economic Journal* (Dec. 1971) in reply to a paper by Prof. E.F. Beach, of McGill University.

I confine myself, in the rest of this note, to the theoretical issue. I shall put the main argument in the form which I prefer; but before I do so it may be well to make a prefatory remark.

Suppose that one approaches the problem in the regular 'neo-classical' manner, begging questions about the meaning of 'capital' in the way that the neo-classics were wont to do. A technical change, if it was to be profitable, must raise the marginal product of at least some factor; but it does not have to raise the marginal products of all factors. Thus, as between two factors, 'labour' and 'capital', it is possible that the marginal products of each may be raised, but it is also possible that that of one factor may be diminished. Thus it is not excluded, in neo-classical terms, that a 'strongly labour-saving invention' may diminish the marginal product of labour. But if it does so, our neo-classic would say, the marginal product of capital must be increased; so profits must be increased. The increase of profits will facilitate accumulation; and an increase in capital, with no further 'labour-saving' change, must increase the marginal product of labour. So it all comes out 'for the best' in the end, just as Ricardo (in his chapter on Machinery) said.

There is indeed a parallelism between this neo-classical argument and Ricardo's. But it is not made at all clear, on the neo-classical approach, just what it is that distinguishes a 'strongly labour-saving invention'. So we cannot tell at all easily whether the strongly labour-saving case is important or not. I believe that that comes out much better on the other approach.

We then think of production, on both 'old' and 'new' techniques, as being divisible into *operations*, each of which contains a constructional stage, in which a plant (or 'machine') is produced, and a utilizational stage, in which the machine is worked to produce final output. The length of time that is occupied by the constructional stage, and the length of time occupied by the utilizational stage, are supposed to be the same on the two techniques. Since the 'machines' are different in kind, there is no technical equivalence between the old machine and the new (how many stage-coaches make a railway train?); they can only be compared by reference to their cost of construction, or by reference to their capacity for producing final output. It does not matter which we use, for exactly the same argument can be written either way. I prefer to work with capacity to produce final output.

A 'machine' is thus defined as a capacity-unit—a piece of equipment which has the capacity to produce (per unit of time) some fixed quantity of final output. Then (if we allow ourselves to confine attention to labour inputs) there are only two ways in which the techniques can differ—in the quantity of labour which is needed to produce the capacity-unit, and in the quantity of labour that is needed to work it. There are just these two parameters, or technical coefficients. They are both of them labour-coefficients; we may call them the construction coefficient and the utilization coefficient respectively.

At the moment when the new technique is introduced, all existing machines are of the old type; they will go on being used as long as it is profitable to use them. But if the new technique (considered as a whole) is more profitable than the old, the newly constructed machines, henceforward, will be of the new type. Gradually, as time goes on, the proportion of new machines in the whole stock of machines will rise.

Since we are supposing that the final product produced by the two techniques is the same (if not physically the same, economically equivalent), it is impossible that the new technique can be more profitable if both of its coefficients are higher. But this still leaves three alternatives open: (1) both coefficients may be lower on the new technique; (2) the construction coefficient may be higher, but the utilization coefficient may be so much lower as to more than compensate; (3) the utilization coefficient may be higher, but the construction coefficient may be so much lower as to more than compensate. All of these alternatives are possible. It is the second which gives rise to the 'Ricardo-machinery effect'.

A simple way of showing this is the following. Consider,

first, as a standard of reference, the completely unbiased improvement, in which both coefficients are reduced, and reduced to exactly the same proportional extent. The change in technique can then occur, with full employment of labour, and without any transfer of labour between sectors. The same labour force, applied to machine-making, will produce more machines (capacity-units); but the labour required to man a machine will be reduced in the same proportion, so that the same labour force which was required to man the old machines will man the new. But the new have a larger capacity, so final output will be increased as soon as the new machines come into use; the rise in final output will be proportional to the number of new machines that have come into use, so there will be an extra output, over and above what there would have been if the 'invention' had not been made, which will gradually rise until it reaches a maximum, at the point when the whole stock of machines consists of new machines.

Contrast with this what happens in the case which is at the boundary between my first and second alternatives. Here there is no saving in constructional labour, but in utilizational labour there is substantial economy. In this case the possibility of increasing output depends upon the transfer of labour between sectors; and it is only the labour which is displaced by the new machines which is available as a source of increased output. No more labour can be employed in making new machines, in an initial period, while the first of the new machines are being constructed, than would have been employed 'otherwise', without a fall in final output during that period (for the only source of such labour, at that stage, is the labour which is still required for working the old machines). If the same labour (as 'otherwise') is employed in making machines *in that period*, the number of machines (capacity-units) which will be produced will *now* be the same as 'otherwise'; so in the next period there will be no increase in final output (where there would have been an increase in the unbiased case). But in this period less labour will be required for utilization, and that labour can be transferred to make possible an increase in output of new machines. This increase in output will usually, however, be rather slow, but in time, as more and more labour is transferred, it will mount up.

In the full 'Ricardian' case, where the construction coefficient is *raised*, the effect just considered is intensified. There must be a transfer of labour, even immediately, if the capacity to produce final output is not to fall (below what it would have been 'otherwise') as the new more expensive machines come into production. But (again assuming Full Employment) there can be no immediate transfer of labour, except at the cost of diminishing current final output, for the available labour is still required to maintain output from the old machines. A stage in which final output is less than it would have been if the change in technique had not occurred is thus inevitable.

[This is really the main thing which I (and I believe Ricardo also) have been trying to say. It is perfectly possible that the adoption of a (profitable) new invention may lead to a (temporary) reduction in final output; the condition which is necessary for this to happen is not particularly stringent, or unrealistic. It does not look like being an 'empty economic box'. As for the further question, of the effect of the reduction on the real wage of labour, I do not mean that it is impossible for the real wage to be unaffected; but if final output (consumption output) is reduced, someone must economize— or an unchanged consumption must be supplied from some other source. There are several such possibilities—increased saving, drawing on stocks, borrowing from abroad; in a complete analysis each of these should be taken into account. But I cannot see that these sources can be counted on—certainly not to do all that is required. If they do not do all that is required, there must be a (temporary) fall in real wages, below what would 'otherwise' have been attainable.]

I hope I have made it clear that I do not hold that these are necessary consequences of 'machinery', or of industrialization. All I am saying is that there are good theoretical reasons for holding that rapid industrialization can quite easily prove to be a strain.

(iv) An addendum to Capital and Time

The main thing which I now feel should have been added to *Capital and Time* (1973) is the concept of the *Impulse*, of which much use has been made in the first and second essays in the present book. I came upon that concept, as a result of writing *Capital and Time*. The relation between the abstract analysis of that work and the Impulse concept, which (as shown above) can be used in a much less abstract fasion, needs, however, some explanation.

It is best to go back to the beginning. As I explained, I was originally led to the idea of resurrecting Böhm-Bawerk (or something like him) by a suggestion that came from Professor C.M. Kennedy. He had observed that it was a serious weakness of the type of analysis which I had used in my *Capital and Growth* (1965)—in the 'Growth Equilibrium' or steady state chapters—that it implied that 'the capital goods produced during a period are themselves used in the production of the output of the period. Such an idea has no meaning in terms of economic reality.'[5] The reproof had clearly to be accepted; but I did not find that the attempt made by Kennedy, to mend my model by introducing lags, but leaving it otherwise unchanged, was very promising. I felt more inclined to 'go the whole Austrian way with Mrs. Robinson', as he put it.

For I had myself already encountered a parallel trouble. Though I had swallowed the timeless, or lagless, formulation in the steady state chapters of *Capital and Growth*, and had not felt much inconvenience in so doing, I did have trouble when I tried to leave the steady state. The embryonic theory of 'Traverse', which I put out in Chapter XVI of that same book, had not satisfied me at all. So I jumped at Kennedy's suggestion, since he seemed to have identified just what it was that had gone wrong with that first 'Traverse' theory.

[5] See his contribution to the book of essays entitled *Value, Capital and Growth* (1968), p. 276.

I saw, however, no reason to follow him in supposing that an 'Austrian' approach involved 'leaving out fixed capital altogether'.[6] For I had myself, long ago, constructed a form of Austrian theory in which there was a place for fixed capital.[7] It was rusting unused, but the time had come to bring it back.

In that version, the version I used in *Capital and Time*, fixed capital goods do appear, but not explicitly. One looks solely at the streams of 'original' inputs and of final outputs. The fixed capital goods are implied, but they are regarded as intermediate products and not shown.

Now it is of course perfectly true that this is not the only way of introducing fixed capital *and* lags. There is a well-established alternative method, the method that was introduced by von Neumann. On the von Neumann method the intermediate products are shown; they are regarded as inputs of the periods in which they are used, and outputs of the periods in which they are constructed. So, at the join, at the turnover from period to period, they come to the surface and have prices put upon them. I have never denied that this is a possible, and for some purposes a fruitful, way of proceeding.

To those who (like the author of the longest review of *Capital and Time* that has yet appeared[8]) are deeply committed to the von Neumann approach, my alternative has seemed to be an intrusion. Why bother us with an alternative when we are quite happy already? I concede that in my opening chapter I did not give a fully sufficient reason. It is not enough to say that universal pricing, at the turnover from period to period, is unrealistic; that many capital goods go on being used for years, within the same firm, without changing hands. That is true, but it is also true that some do get traded, especially at the stage between construction and utilization, but sometimes at other times. If von Neumann over-emphasizes

---

[6] Ibid., p. 289.
[7] *Value and Capital* (1939), ch. XV–XVII.
[8] E. Burmeister, in the *Journal of Economic Literature* (June 1974).

intermediate transactions, I was clearly under-emphasizing them. It was not enough to say that one needed both extremes in order to maintain a 'balance'.

The true justification of the Austrian method is different, but it was only at a much later point in my work that it appeared. It does not appear in the opening chapters which are building up to a statement of steady state conditions. For the fact is that in the steady state, as in the stationary state of the classics, it does not matter what approach one uses; one comes out in much the same place any way. All one gets is a different form of statement, since the things that are allowed to have movements ('virtual' movements) are not quite the same. But there must be consistency, and there must be broad resemblance. So the rules about growth rates and interest rates (which come to the surface in all three approaches) are just the same in a von Neumann model, in the Austrian model, in the lagless *Capital and Growth* model, and no doubt in others. So, if one looks no further than the steady state, there is nothing particular to be claimed for the Austrian approach, save (perhaps) some didactic elegance.[9]

---

[9] Baumeister claims that I could further have improved the elegance of my exposition if I had allowed wages to be paid *post factum* (at the end of the 'week', instead of at the beginning of the 'week', as I did). I would certainly have brought my algebra into closer relation with the work of some steady-statists (such as Sraffa) if I had adopted a *post factum* convention. And it may be admitted that there is nothing more realistic about one of these assumptions than about the other. Inputs are not necessarily paid for at the moment when they are applied, nor outputs at the moment when they are delivered; thus there is an element of loan, which is attached to be the purchase or sale. I nevertheless considered, and I still consider, that these loans, which muddle the time-sequence, should for analytical purposes be disregarded. Inputs are in general applied before outputs are ready; a model like mine, in which production lags are to be given their proper place, should show this. The simplest way of ensuring that one does not miss it is to adopt my *ante factum* convention.

It is true that when I came to the special case of the Simple Profile I modified this a little for ease of exposition. I neglected thie application of utilizational labour in the 'week' before the output stream

But when we leave the steady state, the position is quite different. The true advantage of the Austrian method is that it is much better than its rivals at dealing with Traverse, and so with Innovation. It is admittedly not equally good at dealing with all aspects of Innovation; the effects of innovation upon industrial structure (as reflected in the input–output matrix) are for instance not well shown. Nor is it equally good at dealing with all kinds of innovation; those which involve the introduction of new consumption goods are, formally at least, excluded.[10] It can, however, deal much better than its rivals, with the basic economic effects of what is surely the most important kind of innovation, that which takes the form of new methods for making the same final product. Such innovations, nearly always, involve the introduction of new capital goods, new sorts of 'machines', and of other intermediate products. It is here undesirable that these goods should be physically specified, since there is no way of establishing a physical relation between the capital goods that are required in the one technique and those that are required in the other. The only relation that can be established runs in terms of costs, and of capacity to produce final output; and this is precisely what is preserved in an Austrian theory.

So the subject of Part II (of *Capital and Time*) is the theory of innovation; not the causes of innovation but its effects, the study of the Impulse that an innovation gives. I fully admit that I give no more than the beginnings of such a theory; far too much is left out for more than that to be claimed. There is nothing about money; nothing about monopolies (of labour or of capital); nothing about government; nothing, except in a concluding passage (in Chapter XII), about natural scarcities.

---

begins. But why should one not suppose that the constructional labour (now packing up) should be partially laid off in that 'week'? That would mend this little 'roughness', if it has to be mended.

[10] See, however, *Capital and Time*, pp. 143–6, where it is shown that a link with the problem of new goods in the theory of income measurement can readily, and usefully, be established.

But these (as is shown in preceding essays in the present book[11]) can, at least to some extent, be put back. We still need a model of the innovative process, in itself, to serve as a framework; that is what I was trying to provide.

Many economists would take it for granted that when all these simplifications had been made (or these obstacles, as they might perhaps consider them, had been removed) there must, after a single innovative disturbance, not followed by any other, be a smooth convergence to an equilibrium; and there are growth models which seem to tell the same tale. Mine does not. I do indeed begin with a case (my Standard case) in which it can be proved that there is assured convergence; even that case required a lot of working out. Even there, there is the possibility that technical progress may have drastic, and possibly unacceptable, effects on distribution—the Ricardo machinery effect (for which see above).[12] When we go beyond the standard case, as I did, though not at the same length, the prospects for convergence look less good.

There are at least two further obstacles. One is the possibility of disturbances arising from shortening or lengthening of the production period (the possibility that was first brought to the attention of economists in the *Prices and Production* of Professor Hayek); the other, which I am more inclined to believe to be of realistic importance, is a matter of the time-shape of the normal productive process itself. It turns out that it is only when processes have the convenient time-shape of the Simple Profile that they can be relied upon to fit comfortably together.[13] If the typical process requires more input for its full development than it does at its beginning, then *either* fewer will be started to give continuous full employment *or* processes which have been started will have to be stopped, and cannot be carried through.

---

[11] I refer again to Essays I and II above.
[12] pp. 184–89, above.
[13] *Capital and Time*, pp. 135–7.

When I got that far, I had began to lose interest in convergence. If it had been shown to be dubious, had it not also been
shown to be unimportant? Even at the best, it would take a
long time; and in most applications, before that time had
elapsed, something else (some new exogenous shock) would
have occurred. It was therefore of the first importance that
something could be said, by my method, about the short-run
and medium-run effects of an innovation—what I call the Early
Phase. (In fact, the Early Phase is much easier to deal with
than the Late Phase; and it is only in the Late Phase that any
question of convergence to equilibrium can arise.)

Thus it was that I was led to the concept of the Impulse—
these short-run and medium-run effects becoming one's main
concern. But, it may well be asked, was not this running on
too fast? The Traverse theory, in its Austrian form, had apparently done no more than show what would happen (under
many simplifying assumptions) when a steady state was disturbed by an innovation; the steady state was still there, even
if it was used as no more than a starting-point. Was it justifia-
ble to use it as a starting-point if there was no assurance that
it would ever be reached? I do not think that I have a
complete answer to that objection, but I have a partial answer.
For I did get to the point, in my chapter on Substitution
(which is the principal Impulse chapter), when I could consider the effect of a second technical change occurring *after* a
first.[14] Whether the second change is induced by the economic
consequences of the first, or whether it comes from an independent innovation, does not essentially matter. This nevertheless meant that I could say something, at least, about the
impact of change upon an economy which was not in a steady
state initially. The dependence upon a steady state, somewhere
in the past, is formally still there; but I think I can claim that
at the point thus reached it is on the way out. We can push it
back as far as we like until it does not much matter.

I for one am glad to be rid of it.

[14] *Capital and Time*, pp. 113 ff. See also Mathematical Appendix, pp.
199-202.

INDEX